How to Avoid
BURNOUT

How to Avoid BURNOUT

Timothy Ponder

"Thou wilt keep him in perfect peace, whose mind is stayed on thee; because he trusteth in thee. Trust ye in the Lord for ever: for in the Lord Jehovah is everlasting strength." Isaiah 26:3, 4

Pacific Press Publishing Association
Mountain View, California
Oshawa, Ontario

ISBN 0-8163-0536-6

Dedication

To our baby daughter Rachel, whose sweet little smile is one of the best safeguards I have against burning out.

"God, give us grace to accept with serenity
      the things that cannot be changed,
Courage to change the things which should be changed,
And the wisdom to distinguish the one from the other."

—Niebuhr's "Serenity Prayer" delivered in a service
at the Congregational Church, Heath, Massachusetts, 1943.

Contents

A "Burned-out" Society

"Why am I so miserable if these are the best years of my life?" That question is borrowed from the title of Andrea Eagen's book about the difficult teenage years. Of course, it is a good question many adults should be asking themselves. "I have everything going for me—a good job, a comfortable home, a wonderful family. Why am I an unhappy person? What is missing in my life?"

The media tells us constantly about the good life and how we can achieve success. Most of us strive to reach the ideal of full, successful living. We reach for more and more, but even when we "arrive" at the so-called pinnacle of success, we are still dissatisfied. So often a disenchantment which does not seem to go away sets in about life in general.

At the height of his worldwide fame and wealth, John Lennon cried out in his song "I'm So Tired": "I'd give you everything I've got for a little peace of mind." While millions adored the man, few realized that at the time he was beginning an addiction to heroin which nearly destroyed him. A few years before, Mick Jagger sang what was to become an anthem for a troubled world: "I Can't Get No Satisfaction." If you look past the song's bad grammar and raucous music, we realize that for many it is speaking the truth: "I have tried everything in my life—money, power, sex, intellectualism, the discos, countless other amusements, the human potential movement—I've tried it all, but still have not found any satisfaction."

An emotional malady of staggering consequences is plaguing people throughout the industrialized world. Some call this "new" disease "burnout." It is, at its most basic level, an erosion of the spirit. A "burned-out" person is someone who has invested enormous amounts of energy into making life meaningful for himself and others around him. But unfortunately, he is presently "running on empty." He is working more and enjoying it less. Life, and especially the work environment, is a constant source of inner stress and turmoil. The very aspects of his life which were once joyful, challenging, and satisfying are now intolerable burdens. He needs help, and he is not alone. There are thousands of others like him.

Some have not accepted burnout as a legitimate emotional disorder. However, this does not mean that it is nonexistent. As you continue reading, you probably will discover some of the symptoms of burnout either in yourself or the people with whom you closely associate. The greatest benefit that has come to me from my research for this book is that I have detected within my own life some of the early warning signals of this complex and difficult problem. Consequently, I have been able to formulate a personal strategy for counteracting burnout and for coping with life's pressures and stresses in a more effective way. After all, it would be a shame to find yourself burned out at the age of 27!

Lance Morrow helps us to see the broad scope of the burnout phenomenon: "Today, burnout is a syndrome verging on a trend. The smell of psychological wiring on fire is everywhere. The air-traffic controllers left their jobs in part, they said, because the daily tension tended to scorch out their circuits (the primitive 'flee-or-fight' reaction to danger squirted charges of adrenaline into bodies that had to remain relatively immobile, tethered by duty to scope and computer).

"Burnout runs through the teaching profession like Asian flu— possibly because it depresses people to be physically assaulted by those they are trying to civilize. Two years ago, Willard McGuire, president of the National Education Association, said that burnout among teachers 'threatens to reach hurricane force if it isn't checked soon.' Social workers and nurses burn out from too much association with hopelessness. Police officers burn out. Professional athletes burn out. Students burn out. Executives burn out. Housewives burn out. And, as every parent knows, there usually comes a moment in late afternoon when baby burnout occurs—all of his little circuits overloaded, the child feels too wrought up to fall asleep."[1]

Something definitely has gone wrong somewhere. Jesus came into this world so "that they might have life, and that they might have it more abundantly." John 10:10. Why are so many people, including committed Christians, falling victim to the emotional malaise of the 1980s? *How to Avoid Burnout* will raise some new questions in your mind, as well as seek to answer them. Ideally, it will provide some new insights to you if your life is stressful. However, don't expect to find all the answers here, or in any other book which has a human author. No one has all the answers. But if you read this book, along with some of the books listed in the section of the book titled "For Further Reading," you will have a better understanding of how to avoid burnout. Four tests and inventories about burnout and its precursor, stress, are found in the following pages. Pay special attention to them, because they will help you know yourself better.

Above all, don't neglect the inspired Source of counsel.

Many inspirational writers have shown how Christian principles incorporated into our lives can help reduce the impact of stress. A right knowledge of these foundation principles can provide stability and happiness in our lives. One Christian writer, Ellen G. White, has particularly relevant counsel. Some of these thoughts are included in this book. Most important, we should realize that the Bible contains all of the foundation principles which are able to provide us stability and happiness in our lives. This book will highlight these principles throughout its pages. If we choose to implement these principles into our lives, then we will be like the house which Jesus describes in the Sermon on the Mount: "And the rain descended, and the floods came, and the winds blew, and beat upon that house; and it fell not: for it was founded upon a rock." Matthew 7:25.

1. *Time*, 21 September 1981, p. 84.

People Just Like You

What type of people is encountering burnout today? It may come as a shock, but they are common ordinary people—folks just like you or me. They are not mystics, criminals, or psychotics. Instead, the victim of burnout is hardworking and dedicated, sincere and loyal—at least he begins that way. He or she is someone you would welcome to live next door to you.

What are burned-out people like? What inner turmoils and anxieties do they go through? You'll have to wait until the next chapter to get a comprehensive description of burnout. Instead, to answer these questions we will first take a look at five true-to-life illustrations of people who have burned out in varying degrees and for varying reasons. Their stories are not unique. There are those around you who could tell similar stories. Perhaps you will be able to identify with some of their emotions and struggles.

THE BATTERED TEACHER

Silvia Rodriguez, thirty-five, called it quits after ten years in the Connecticut school system. It wasn't because of a lack of dedication; she just couldn't take it anymore. Silvia worked hard to be a good teacher. She wrote her own class materials for her high school courses so that they would be more interesting. She devoted herself to civic causes such as the March of Dimes walkathon and the Special Olympics for handicapped children. This quite often meant the sacrifice of a weekend, time she would rather have spent at home. Despite all of the hard work, she felt that no one appreciated her or her efforts. She felt the school administrators and the community just ignored her and took her for granted.

In the spring of 1979 came the moment of truth. She was wounded while trying to break up a fight between two students in her classroom. She was hurt, both physically and psychologically, "I went home and began feeling very sick. I was out of school for three weeks. My body was in a lot of pain. I began looking at myself and I realized it was not worthwhile. I was increasingly tired, increasingly bored. The thought of having to go back to teach was very scary, very petrifying. I really had a tremendous fear when I went back to the classroom. When I realized I had lost the trust of my students and that I was not feeling comfortable in their company any longer, I decided they did not need me."

Mrs. Rodriguez left the teaching profession in June 1979 and now is happily employed at the National Institute of Education in Washington as an advisor on youth education and employment programs. She does not wish ever again to enter the classroom as a teacher of high school students.[1]

BURNOUT IN THE DENTIST'S OFFICE

Joseph, forty-five, is a dentist. Most people would take one quick look at Joseph and say that he has it made. His office is in a fashionable suite in a medical office building. He seems to have all the money and possessions he could ever hope for. He lives in an exclusive country subdivision within a twenty-minute drive of his office. To the casual observer, Joseph's work appears easy and nonstressful. Of course, dentistry requires much skill, but Joseph does not face the tensions encountered by his close friend who is a heart surgeon. Few people die in a dentist chair (although some may think they will). One other factor seems to be in his favor: he is his own boss and can set up his own schedule. No one tells him what hours he should practice; he has much more autonomy and freedom than most other health professionals.

Therefore, it probably comes as a surprise that Joseph and many others in the dental profession are experiencing burnout. Suicide is more common among dentists, per capita, than among any other profession.[2] Several factors account for Joseph's stress and resulting burnout. The first one is the fear and anxiety exhibited by his patients. Very seldom does he get a patient who is looking forward to seeing him. It is even rarer for a patient to express appreciation for a good filling or a good extraction. Instead, most patients in his office want to get out of his office as soon as they possibly can. The only time he ever hears from them is when they have some sort of complaint.

The cost of Joseph's suite and equipment is quite high. His total overhead runs from between 70 to 80 percent of what he collects from patients. Because of this fact, Joseph is tempted to schedule more patients per day than he has in the past. This only tends to make work in his office more hectic and stressful. At the same time, Joseph is affected by feelings of boredom and loneliness. He performs many routine tasks of dentistry all day long. Certainly, he performs those tasks very well because of his specialized training. However, the repetitive nature of his work causes him to occasionally get bored. His loneliness stems from the fact that no one is around who is willing to express appreciation for his ability as a dentist or who can give him advice and assistance when it is needed. He feels professionally isolated.

For this and other reasons, Joseph is exhibiting many of the symptoms found in the burnout syndrome. The most obvious one to his wife is his drinking. She worries about this, because she knows this has had an adverse effect upon their marriage. She thinks to herself, "If his patients found out about his drinking, it could wreck his career." But Joseph is not all that worried about preserving it. In fact, he hopes within a few years to become financially independent enough to get out of dentistry altogether. He is pouring more and more of his assets into his real estate investments. He is counting on these financial ventures to be his ticket out of the dental profession and into an early retirement.[3]

A PASTOR IN TROUBLE

John, thirty-two, is what the church administration would consider a model pastor. Each year he has exceeded their expectations for productivity: he has had a good number of new members coming into his church; his church has shown a healthy tithe increase; he has demonstrated time and again his strong, effective church leadership. The evangelistic meetings he conducted the previous autumn were very successful, with many new accessions to the church membership as a result of them. The members all remarked that their church had been blessed in a special way. Church services are more enthusiastic than ever, especially after the pastor attended a church-growth seminar and learned some new ideas about the worship experience. John's sermons are known throughout the region for being dynamic and full of spiritual food. He works hard at being a pastor; many days he's up at six in the morning and does not stop until eleven in the evening. The members and his superiors admire his vigor and dedication.

But take a look inside his home. After John removes his mask of pastoral charm and pleasantness, he comes home to his family. Here John often reveals himself to be an angry, frustrated, and hostile man. His inner hostility and frustration come from many sources: church goals and the pressures to achieve them, the seemingly endless number of personal problems which he confronts in his visitation program, the feeling that he and his family are constantly under review and scrutiny, the unrelenting busyness of his schedule. He tries to please everyone, but there is always criticism and complaints—some of them personal attacks leveled against him and his church program.

He knows a pastor is expected to stay calm at all times. He can't yell. Therefore he takes out his frustrations upon his family. He and his wife are having many more arguments than usual, often over trivial matters. These disputes almost always become bitter confrontations that resolve little. Several times his wife has thought of consulting a marriage counselor, but John has talked her out of it. After all, how would it look for a pastor and his wife to receive marriage counseling!

Over the past several months John has tended to keep his own children at arm's length, preferring to spend long periods of time locked in his study. While he maintains the appearance of a busy pastor, he tries to spend as much time away from his parishioners and interested persons as he can. He watches a lot of TV and reads many light newsstand magazines in an effort to relax, but his wife notices with concern that her husband always acts restless. One thing John, the pastor, is not doing very much of at all is deep, meditative Bible study and prayer. He blames this on his busy schedule. This pattern of neglecting spiritual devotion began about a year ago, during the hectic evangelistic campaign. At first the pattern bothered him, but now he's become used to it. If only he could realize that here is the source of his restless, troubled spirit.

While John's wife is concerned about her husband, she does not know everything about him. John has a serious psychological hang-up which no one, not even his wife, knows about. His developing burnout has pushed him into a sinful activity which he indulged in before his conversion. John began several months ago to frequent adult bookstores and pornographic movie theaters. He realizes that if his problem is ever discovered it could mean the end of his ministry, but his burnout is so far advanced that he doesn't really care anymore. John is living a double life: on one level he is playing the role of a busy, successful, inspiring spiritual leader. On another level he is a wretched individual filling his mind with a constant stream of wickedness as he aimlessly spends his afternoons in darkened theaters. He questions both his Christian experience and his sanity. At times he desperately wants to pull out of the awful quagmire he finds himself in, but he discovers that he can't.

John does not realize it, but the days of his ministry are numbered. Unknown to John, the negative mental conditioning of the past four months is setting him up to fall headlong into an illicit affair. At the right time and place, evil forces will present to his mind a temptation which will be overpowering to him. The result—a wrecked ministry and a wrecked family, along with a disillusioned church and community.[4]

THE BURNED-OUT MARRIAGE

Dina is a middle-aged woman whose marriage of fourteen years fell apart. One day she shared her feelings with a discussion group at a burnout workshop. She shows to us that burnout can happen inside the marriage relationship, as well as in other areas of life outside of our work environment. Notice how she describes the breakdown between herself and her husband: ''I feel hollow in this relationship. There is nothing between us: no bond, no communication, no sharing, no contact, no feelings, nothing. We have no plans together, no interests together. The tensions are making me tired and sad. There is no hope for us. There is nothing that he does to enhance my life in any way, either emotionally, intellectually, or physically. I don't feel like a couple, I feel emotionally deprived. I feel resentful and irritated. I have to close myself off emotionally to stop feeling that way. I can't give myself sexually or emotionally to him anymore. I don't believe life has anything to give me. I would do anything to be free of him.''[5]

BURNOUT AT AN EARLY AGE

Nancy had been named after her aunt, her mother's sister. Her aunt had been a brilliant woman, a virtuosa pianist. Unfortunately, the woman died in her late twenties, not long before Nancy's birth. Because of the close emotional bond between the two sisters, Nancy's mother sought to keep her sister's memory alive through her child. Nancy, was constantly told stories about her aunt—how smart, talented, and pretty she had been and how every little girl should aspire to be just like her.

Nancy began piano lessons at the age of four. Her mother urged her to practice for lengthy periods so that she could play beautifully, ''just like Aunt Nancy used to.'' As she grew older, Nancy practiced increasingly from a sense of duty. She secretly hated to practice, but she wanted to make her mother happy. As a result of her hard work, she did become proficient on the piano. However, she dreaded the numerous recitals: both the public ones and those which her mother arranged at home to show off Nancy's talents in front of the family's friends.

Nancy also felt the pressure to perform at school. Aunt Nancy had had almost a flawless academic career. But Nancy found the studies at school not all that easy. She was just an average student. So, the constant pressure from her parents caused her to be burdened down. She could not enjoy her high school experience. At the age of fifteen, Nancy suffered from what the psychologist described as a nervous breakdown. She quit functioning as a normal adolescent and became a rebellious, noncommunicative truant. Her parents could not understand what was causing her to lash out against them. They thought that they had provided everything she needed to be a happy and successful young woman. "Why is she acting this way?" was their agonizing question. They failed to see the role they had played, nor had they seen the early warning signals of burnout—"sadness, medical blackouts, unnatural fatigue, the beginning abuse of alcohol."[6]

We have taken a close look at burnout through the perspective of personal experiences. These cases show us how burnout did its work in the lives of five individuals. Now we are ready to take a systematic and in-depth look at burnout: what it is, what its symptoms are, and whether you yourself are experiencing certain elements of this phenomenon. We'll do this as we examine "a profile of a victim."

1. *The Sunday Oklahoman*, 5 April 1981.

2. Rosalind Forbes, *Corporate Stress* (Garden City, New York: Doubleday, 1979), p. 187.

3. This is a composite illustration. The information used in writing it came from Ayala Pines and Elliot Aronson, *Burnout: From Tedium to Personal Growth* (New York: Free Press, 1981), pp. 6-9, and Rosalind Forbes, *Corporate Stress*, pp. 187, 188.

4. This is a composite illustration. The information used in writing it came from being acquainted with several burned-out ministers, although key components of their experiences have been changed to protect their identity and save them from embarrassment.

5. *Pines and Aronson*, p. 181.

6. Herbert J. Freudenberger with Geraldine Richelson, *Burnout: How to Beat the High Cost of Success* (New York: Bantam Books, 1981), pp. 25, 26.

Profile of a Victim

One April morning I heard the news that the school gym had been gutted with fire the night before. An investigation determined a few days later that a stuck thermostat caused the fire. The thermostat failed to adequately regulate the heater; the heater got hotter and hotter until a fire resulted. Smoke damage was extensive in the kitchen and the gym.

A week after the fire I drove by the school to survey the damage. The outside shell looked fairly normal, because the walls had been constructed of brick and concrete blocks. The corrugated metal roof also seemed to be mostly intact. But the windows showed dark streaks of black soot. Several were broken. It was only when I looked inside that I saw the real tragedy. Utter devastation—ashes, soot, and charred pieces of wood.

Just a few days before this place had been full of laughter, games, and activity. Now it stood, dark, forbidding, and lonely. Only a day before the fire I had finished giving a week of prayer series there to the elementary children.

Psychologists and counselors are beginning to realize that people, as well as buildings, "burn out." The curious thing about many people is that they are like the burned-out gym: when you look at their exterior selves, nothing much appears to have changed. It is only when you get the chance to take a glimpse into their inner selves that you can view the utter devastation caused by the strains and stresses of living. Their lives are being spent in silent desperation. The inner resources needed for joyful, vibrant living have been consumed.

Dr. Herbert J. Freudenberger coined the word *burnout* to describe the nameless malaise which he and those around him had suffered. Whenever he shared the term and concept with both patients and colleagues, he met with immediate identification. They would say "Yeah, that's how I feel—burned out." They knew exactly what he was talking about. This psychologist from New York wrote a definitive book on the subject, *Burn Out: How to Beat the High Cost of Success*. Dr. Ayala Pines and Elliot Aronson have written another in-depth, well-documented volume called *Burnout: From Tedium to Personal Growth*. Dr. Christiana Maslach, professor of psychology at the University of California at Berkeley, is another important name to remember in burnout research. These last three researchers have approached burnout mainly from the standpoint of one's occupation or profession, while Freudenberger presents burnout as a problem which threatens every aspect of life. These and other psychologists bring to us many valuable insights, some of which are presented in this book. However, it is vitally important that Christians analyze their ideas carefully. Some of their concepts fit harmoniously with the Christian world view; others reflect their humanistic background and are therefore in opposition to Christian principles.

If the phenomenon of burnout could be reduced to one word, what would it be? Perhaps the best one to use would be *exhaustion*. This exhaustion comes as a result of the depletion of inner resources. The burned-out state finds us "running on empty." Practically every one of us at some time has let his car run out of gas. Of course, we are warned ahead of time by a gas-gauge needle leaning perilously to the left. It registers "empty," but the engine continues to run for a number of miles. This fact may cause us to have a false sense of security. We may decide to take a chance, believing we can make it to our favorite station. But then the engine sputters and misses, finally refusing to run altogether. It has run out of gas.

This analogy of "running on empty" is a helpful one in understanding burnout. When a person begins to burn out, many early warning signals or symptoms should become apparent. These warning signals grow more intense as time moves forward. What are these warning signals? What are they telling the person? The spiritual, emotional, and physical resources he needs for daily living are becoming depleted. The person has two choices: do something in response to those warning signals, or ignore them. If he does ignore them, various facets of life will slowly begin to falter and unravel. At its farthest extreme, burnout causes the person to collapse in total exhaustion. He might even suffer from stress-related illnesses that will threaten his very life.

Burnout, therefore, is a serious matter which should not be ignored. The exhaustion which burnout causes exhibits itself on three fronts: *physical, emotional,* and *mental* exhaustion.[1] Typically, the burned-out person will suffer from these different forms of exhaustion simultaneously. That is, some symptoms of physical, mental, and emotional exhaustion will be present alongside each other.

SYMPTOMS OF BURNOUT

A physically exhausted person may suffer from fatigue, weariness, nausea, and frequent headaches. Very often a person can feel physically drained even when he has not exerted himself physically. He probably will be extremely weary at the end of the day, but at the same time be unable to fall asleep. His burnout may even cause him to suffer from frequent nightmares. The subject of his frightening dreams will reflect the problems and tensions he faces during his waking hours. He wakes up the next morning disoriented and tired, before the pressures of the new day have even begun. He wishes he could stay in bed all day.

Emotional exhaustion exhibits itself in feelings of hopelessness and depression. The emotionally exhausted person in extreme cases may show signs of mental illness and begin thinking about suicide. To him the future looks bleak and hopeless. His past appears as wasted years. The emotional energy that once made him feel alive and vibrant has slowly ebbed away. He has reached the point where even his family and friends seem to be a heavy burden, rather than a source of strength and help. The person depleted of his emotional energy will often cry unexpectedly and for no apparent reason. Other emotional cues can help a friend, relative, or co-worker realize that someone close to them may be suffering from burnout. When someone yells and screams in situations where they have previously been calm, or when he laughs at inappropriate moments, we can know that all is not well with that person. He is probably suffering from burnout.

Mental exhaustion can be seen in a person's negative thought patterns. He may have a low self-concept. Feelings of inferiority and inadequacy prevail in his life. "I'm no good. I can't do anything right. I am a failure." Pessimism, the feeling that things can only get worse at work and at home, will constantly color his thoughts. He may think negatively about those around him. Their bad points and faults receive his continual attention. This cynicism about the actions, motives, and words of others follows hand in hand with pessimism.

In addition, professionals in the human services (the "helping professions") who burn out tend to develop dehumanizing attitudes toward those they are trying to serve. Dehumanization is defined as "a decreased awareness of the human attributes of others and a loss of humanity in interpersonal interactions."[2] The professional tends to withdraw from the client or customer which he once gladly served. His past interactions with those persons have left him emotionally and mentally drained. One woman summed up her feelings this way: "The more I'm around those people, the more I like my dog."

OTHER SYMPTOMS OF BURNOUT

1. Increased use of alcohol, food, or drugs. These are used as emotional crutches which the person chooses to lean upon in the hope that they will help block out the emotional pain which certain aspects of his life is causing him.[3]

2. Talk of "the great escape." This might mean moving to some exotic new place or changing to a completely different line of work. For example, the burned-out accountant will talk of farming in Nebraska, or the Dallas attorney dreams of moving to a Caribbean island. The person desires freedom from the hassles of his present existence.[4]

3. Withdrawal from family and friends. Because of his personal crisis, the person tends to become absorbed with his own little world. He has less ability to demonstrate warmth, tenderness, and patience to those who should mean the most to him.[5]

4. Difficulty or inability to concentrate while studying or listening. The mind invariably wanders away from its present focus.

5. Avoid contact with people. A burned-out professional in human services will find himself getting involved in legitimate, nonperson-oriented projects. He does this so that he can retreat from his major task—that of staying close to the needs of the people he is supposed to serve.

6. Experiences "information overload." A person's job requires him to be responsible for huge amounts of technical information, details, and facts. As he focuses his mind each day upon this vast sea of words and figures, he may grow tense and exhausted because his mental faculties have been stretched beyond realistic limits.

7. Late arrival at meetings and appointments or forgetting them altogether.[6]

8. Feelings of resentment and hostility for the employing organization. He thinks, "Everything in the world is controlling me except me. I have no time to do what would be enjoyable to me. I am a slave to the bureaucratic system. I'm tired of working so hard just to make my superiors look good." Conflicts that inevitably arise between one's work and homelife will help add fuel to the already-hot flames of hostility.

Certain symptoms of the burnout syndrome vary, according to the individual. For example, some people will not be able to sleep at night; others will want to sleep for ten hours or more, which is also detrimental to health. Burnout causes many to grow apathetic about their jobs. They are working only for the paycheck and are not seeking any fulfillment or satisfaction for a job well done. Burnout pushes others into becoming genuine workaholics. They work harder and harder, while often getting less and less accomplished. The act of working harder, they hope, will alleviate their many frustrations and anxieties. Such individuals truly "lose themselves in their work."

What many fail to realize is that burnout has a serious impact upon the spiritual life of the Christian.[7] Of course, the cause-to-effect relationship here is circular: the lack of spirituality in a person leads to burnout.

EFFECT OF BURNOUT ON SPIRITUAL LIFE

Impending burnout will endanger one's spiritual life. Jesus tells us in the parable of the sower that the word of God will grow in the hearts of those who are symbolized as being in the good soil. However, the parable tells of thorns which grew up in one part of the field and choked out the tender plant of spirituality. And what do these thorns represent? They stand for "the cares of this world, and the deceitfulness of riches." Matthew 13:22. Certainly these are two stress-producers which cause many to burn out today. These people let Satan's "thornbushes" choke out their prayer life, the one communication line they have with heaven. Bible reading and meditation becomes a meaningless form, which gradually falls victim to their busy, frenzied schedule.

Church attendance endures longer than anything, for the sake of preserving a good appearance. However, the worship experience is not bringing them any inner joy and happiness. They would rather be anywhere else than in church on Sabbath morning. Burnout in the spiritual life sooner or later causes a person to reject long-established moral values and standards. He may begin drinking, swearing, or carrying on an illicit affair. Usually he will seek at first to practice his new set of standards under a cloak of secrecy so that no one will discover his activity. Finally, though, he announces to the world that he is tired of being a hypocrite and of leading a double life. He reveals his new life-style, which usually shocks his friends and loved ones. They can't understand how he could change so radically "overnight." But the metamorphosis really did not happen overnight; it was all a part of a downward process which took months and years to complete.

We have seen that burnout leaves many disenchanted and disillusioned with their marriages and careers—with life in general. In addition, it leaves some dead. What a waste of human potential! The truth is that it does not have to be this way. Someone has said, "You cannot be reduced to ashes unless you were once aflame." God's will is that each one of us be aflame for Him, and He will help us rekindle that spark which perhaps has gone out of our day-to-day experience.

Remember this: burnout does not attack the losers and the lazy, slothful members of society. Instead, its most likely victim is the highly motivated, hardworking achiever. The man or woman with high ideals and a dream of a better tomorrow—this person is the most likely candidate to eventually experience burnout. As Dr. Freudenberger says, "The more I studied, the more I came to realize that Burnout was robbing our society of what it could least afford to lose: high achievers, the men and women of action and purpose to whom the rest of us looked for leadership and inspiration. They were not failure-oriented or habitually self-destructive people. On the contrary, they were the ones most likely to succeed."[8]

DON'T BE A FAILURE

So take heart if you feel that you are one of burnout's victims. Don't consider yourself to be a failure! The rest of your life lies ahead of you, and it has the potential for being much brighter than your past.

By now, you most likely are asking yourself, "Just how severe is *my* condition? Am I near the point of total collapse, or am I experiencing just the beginning symptoms of burnout? Could it be that I have little to worry about? Of course, this book cannot precisely diagnose your condition. You may need the expertise of a trained counselor or psychologist. (If you are a Christian you will want to seek the advice of a Christian professional, so that the answers he gives you will be consistent with your Christian values and principles.)

Although this book cannot diagnose precisely, the following inventory should prove helpful in giving you an idea about the intensity of your suspected burnout, whether it is mild or severe. Answer the questions truthfully; at the same time, however, don't be too pessimistic or rough on yourself. You still have time to do something about it.

ARE YOU BURNING OUT?*

Look back over the past six months. Have you noticed changes in your life in the following areas? Allow 30 seconds for each answer, then assign it a number from 1 (for little or no change) to 5 (for a great deal of change). These changes might manifest themselves in the office, family, or social situations.

____ 1. Do you tire more easily? Feel fatigued rather than energetic?

____ 2. Are people annoying you by telling you, "You don't look so good lately"?

____ 3. Are you working harder and harder and accomplishing less and less?

____ 4. Are you increasingly cynical and disenchanted?

____ 5. Are you often invaded by a sadness you can't explain?

____ 6. Are you forgetting? (appointments, deadlines, personal possessions)

____ 7. Are you increasingly irritable? More short tempered? More disapppointed in the people around you?

____ 8. Are you seeing close friends and family members less frequently?

____ 9. Are you too busy to do even routine things like taking phone calls or reading reports or sending out your Christmas cards?

____10. Are you suffering from physical complaints? (aches, pains, headaches, a lingering cold)

____11. Do you feel disoriented when the activity of the day comes to a halt?

___12. Is joy elusive?

___13. Are you unable to laugh at a joke about yourself?

___14. Does sex seem like more trouble than it's worth?

___15. Do you have very little to say to people?

> Scale: 0-25 You're doing fine
> 26-30 There are things you should be watching
> 36-50 You're a candidate
> 51-65 You are burning out
> over 65 You're in a dangerous place, threatening to your physical and mental well-being.

*"Are You Burning Out?" from *Burn Out* Herbert J. Freudenberger. Copyright © 1980 by Herbert J. Freudenberger, Ph.D. Reprinted by permission of Doubleday & Company, Inc.

1. This section on physical, emotional, and mental exhaustion is condensed and adapted from Ayala Pine's and Elliot Aronson's, *Burnout: From Tedium to Personal Growth*, (New York: Free Press, 1981), pp. 17-21.
2. *Ibid,* p. 19.
3. Marilyn M. Kennedy, *Career Knockouts: How to Battle Back* (New York: Warner Books, 1980), p. 212.
4. *Ibid,* p. 212.
5. *Ibid,* p. 212, 213.
6. Numbers 5, 6, 7 are from Kevin Howse, "When the Pastor Burns Out," *Ministry,* April 1981, p. 29.
7. *Ibid,* p. 29.
8. Herbert J. Freudenberger with Geraldine Richelson, *Burnout: How to Beat the High Cost of Success* (New York: Bantam Books, 1981), p. xvii.

Adding Fuel to the Flames

We need to realize that burnout does not happen to us without a cause. For that reason, it is important that the major causes of burnout be examined. This chapter takes a look at the three top causes—stress, working in the "helping professions," the spiritual factor. There may be certain contributing factors to the burnout syndrome which are not included in the next few pages. However, each case of burnout will, without fail, have at least one of these factors in operation. Often a person will suffer from all three. Recognizing them is important. If you are aware of the enemy's battle plan, it is always easier to gain a victory.

STRESS, A MAJOR FACTOR

Stress is described as "a precursor to burnout."[1] The pressures that stress places upon our bodies and minds lead directly to the state of exhaustion and erosion of spirit described previously. Stress is being blamed today, though, for more than just discomfort, exhaustion, and a lack of peace. If that was all stress did to us, it would be bad enough. However, stress is thought of as the unseen culprit responsible for the development of many health-damaging or life-threatening illnesses: migrain headaches, peptic ulcers, back problems, arthritis, heart disease, even cancer. Randall Schuler, writing in *Your Life and Health*, claims that this silent killer is snuffing out the lives of 650,000 people each year.[2] He mentions some of the diseases listed above as contributing to that figure, and also accuses stress of being responsible, at least in part, for the approximately 14,000 people killed each year in industrial accidents. If this is true we have quite a killer on our hands! Clearly, something must be done about it.

Medical science as a whole realizes the destructive potential of stress, and for that reason, stress research has become one of the most rapidly growing areas in the medical field today. An avalanche of books on the subject is available, but practically all of them reach the same conclusions of the founder of modern stress research, Dr. Hans Selye. His four decades of work in the laboratory produced such books as the landmark volume *The Stress of Life*. Because of that book's technical nature, it perhaps would be advisable for you to read another one of his books first, *Stress Without Distress*. Here he breaks down his major concepts so that the average person can understand them. (Other good books on this subject are listed in the section "For Further Reading.")

Dr. Selye defines stress this way: *"Stress is the nonspecific response of the body to any demand made upon it."*[3] Whenever the body encounters a stressful situation, it must adapt itself. It does not really matter what the source of the stress is. The effect is pretty much the same; the body goes through its process of adaptation. Says Dr. Selye, "Sitting in a dentist's chair is stressful, but so is exchanging a passionate kiss with a lover."[4] Stress can be physical, caused by pain, heat, cold, a dangerous, life-threatening situation; or emotional, caused by joy, sorrow, anger, hatred. Whenever something places demands upon the body, it produces stress within it.

Another definition by Selye may be clearer than the previous one. Stress, he says, is essentially *the wear and tear of living*.[5] We can never escape from this stress, or "wear and tear," except when we die. For that reason, *stress elimination* is an unrealistic goal. However, *stress reduction and management* is realistic and vitally important for our well-being.

The human body has a mechanism built into it which responds to those demands placed upon it daily. This mechanism produces an identifiable biochemical reaction each time it is triggered. Here's what happens in this "fight-or-flight" mechanism, also known as the adaptation response to stress: the source of stress produces an initial alarm reaction, caused by the stimulation of the body's defenses. The body prepares itself for action by pumping extra adrenaline and noradrenaline into the bloodstream. As our bodies react to stress, the pulse and heartbeat quicken, temperature and blood pressure rise, and the digestion slows.

A certain amount of stress is desirable; it does give us a zest for living, if it is managed properly. Our creativity and performance can be maintained at a higher level if a tolerable level of stress is present in our daily existence; just ask any concert pianist or professional ball player.

Although stress can be useful to us, it becomes a destructive force in our lives when it becomes *distress*—a heavy level of stress which taxes us beyond our coping limits. The adaptation response to stress described above does not hurt us unless we permit it to occur on a continual, prolonged basis. Several stress factors may be tolerable by themselves. However, when they are piled up on top of each other, they can produce a level of stress most unbearable.

Stress is managed effectively when we recognize the sources of stress in our life and then find positive ways in which to relate to them. What are the different stress factors in our daily lives and in our environment? Many pages could be devoted to this subject alone. But for the purpose of our study, please take note of the chart of page 35, "Daily Stressors." In this chart, stress sources are divided into seven areas, with the precentage breakdown given for each one.

WORK, A STRESS PRODUCER

Heading the list of stress producers is work. For the average person, work accounts for almost half of his stress in the course of a day. This should not be surprising. Long, intense meetings, deadlines, and constant interruptions from phone calls—they all take their toll. The fear of being laid off due to a slow economy is also very real to many workers today.

Studies have shown that some occupations are measurably more stressful than others. They are that way simply because of the responsibilities or interpersonal contacts which come with the job. Responsibility for the handling of money and valuable documents causes many people to become stressed. But it has been determined that a job which involves responsibility for the welfare and safety of people is one of the most stressful of all.[6] For an air traffic controller, one mistake can be deadly. Because he is responsible for so many lives, a near-miss of two aircraft will have the same impact upon the controller's stress level as if there had actually been a crash. For that reason, ulcers abound. In a busy airport like Chicago-O'Hare, two thirds of the controllers at any given time will be suffering from ulcers. At a busy, metropolitan airport such a job is only held from two to five years; the stress gets to be too much to handle. There are other occupations where stress (for obvious reasons) plays a major role: college and professional sports coaches, stockbrokers, firefighters, policemen, operating room nurses, dentists, and social workers.[7]

Whether we realize it or not, our relationships with our friends and the responsibilities involved in running our homes are quite stressful; together they contribute to almost one fourth of our daily stress.

No one wants to be left friendless. The fear of losing friends, respect, or social standing will cause many to invest large amounts of time and emotional energy into this area of life. Arguments, disagreements, and interpersonal conflicts are especially stress-producing for most of us.

Then there is our daily traveling. It creates almost one tenth of our total stress. For those who daily commute on congested streets and freeways, traveling can cause them to become emotionally drained even before they begin their workday. Traffic jams cause extra stress, especially if one has been late in starting out and/or is supposed to be somewhere in a few minutes. Take note of the items on the chart under the headings "Educational," "Family," and "Miscellaneous."

ENVIRONMENTAL FACTORS AS STRESS PRODUCERS

Various environmental factors, not listed on this chart, should be mentioned. Stress levels are often elevated quite dramatically among those living in urban, industrialized regions. Noise pollution is a major, hidden threat to people's well-being. One writer describes the problem this way: "We are constantly bombarded by a multiplicity of sounds. Some we are aware of; others we have come to accept and barely recognize, despite the fact that all sound has an effect upon us. On city streets the automobile with its honking horns and engine noises, the rumble of trucks, the cacophony of jack hammers and riveters have contributed to the reasons for the exodus from the cities. In the suburbs, new noises are found; the roar of the lawnmower, the whine of power tools, the bombardment of noise in the kitchen from dishwashers, blenders, exhaust fans, disposals, and washing machines, and the roar of airplanes as they approach landing fields."[8] The impact of noise upon the human organism has caused Dr. Vern Knudsen to declare, "Noise is a slow agent of death."[9]

THE EFFECTS OF OVERCROWDING

Overcrowding in cities has been determined to be stressful, and statistics show that Americans tend to crowd together. New York and Los Angeles metropolises have approximately 7 percent of the people in this country; the ten largest metropolitan areas of America contain a little less than a quarter of the population; overall, almost 74 percent live in urban areas and surrounding suburbs. Almost everyone lives under conditions of high population density. Boston, Chicago, New York, and San Francisco each have 10,000 inhabitants per square mile.

What effect does this overcrowding have upon people? Not all the findings are in, although overcrowding experiments with mice and rats have produced some very interesting results: aggressiveness increases, some become reclusive and no longer engage in any social behavior; homosexuality and indiscriminate mating increase. An overall breakdown in normal social behavior is seen. In addition, the adrenal activity in the animals increases—the same mechanism that occurs in human's stress response.[10] Humans in overcrowded situations tend to behave in similar patterns, although some will deny any correlation between the behavior of the two groups. No wonder the rate of major crimes in big cities is five times that of small cities, eight times as great as in the suburbs, and eleven times that of rural areas.[11] The issues of stressful living and exposure to crime are both strong arguments in favor of moving to a rural setting.

Beyond these environmental considerations, several other stress producers, seemingly beyond our control, exist in today's world. The threat of wars and nuclear annihilation is the concern of many. Inflation and other woes of a failing economy always lurk in the background of our lives. The rapid rate of change within our society's institutions has caused a crushing weight of stress on millions, as demonstrated by Alvin Toffler in his book *Future Shock*.

With all these sources of stress, we can see the true reason why Jesus told his disciples, concerning the last days, "And there shall be signs in the sun, and in the moon, and in the stars; and upon the earth distress of nations, with perplexity; the sea and the waves roaring; *men's hearts failing them for fear, and for looking after those things which are coming on the earth:* for the powers of heaven shall be shaken." Luke 21:25, 26, emphasis supplied.

As we grow older, the fact of our own mortality becomes a source of stress for most people. The thought hits us, "I'm not going to be around here forever; someday my life will end." That thought often frightens the older person. Often he will do one of two things: He will either brood constantly about his impending death, or he will seek to repress such thoughts. It is quite possible that the lives of many individuals are shortened because of this overwhelming fear of death!

HOLMES'S THEORY

Thomas Holmes, a University of Washington physician, along with some of his associates, has developed the Social Readjustment Rating Scale. This scale shows the amount of stress involved in various life events. Dr. Holmes observed over 5000 patients and discovered that illness and disease very often came to them after some event or a combination of events had occurred which forced them to adapt in a radical way. He observed that certain events have a greater impact upon a person's life than other events. For example, a traffic ticket or Christmas holiday will cause some stress and need for adaptation, although it will be slight. However, a divorce, jail term, or being fired from work will be much more traumatic. The highest event he placed on his scale is the death of a spouse.[12]

As a result of his research, Holmes ranked the life events which bring change into our lives and assigned to each one of them an LCU—a "life change unit" point. This relative ranking of events includes both what we consider good and bad events in our lives. Both bring extra stress to us. Marriage, moving to a new home, joining a new church, getting a better job—all of these bring stress and change into our lives, even though we consider them to be good or happy events. This explains why many young stars soon fall apart emotionally; they simply cannot deal with the rapid change of life which instant fame has brought to them.

Holmes's theory, then, is that too much change in our lives often is accompanied by the greater chance of illness or accident. For your benefit, this scale is on page 37. Test yourself. According to Holmes, if your total score is below 150 points, you will have one chance in three of a serious health change in the next two years. If your score is between 150 and 300, your chances rise to 50-50. A score of more than 300 points means that your chances rise to 80 percent or more of having a serious health problem within several years. Although this is just a theory, it is one based upon the experiences of many people. Holmes's advice: Try to space out those life events which you anticipate and control.[13]

DAILY STRESSORS*

Work Related (47% of all daily stressors)
1. Monotonous, repetitive tasks such as assembly line work, clerical, or typing jobs
2. Work-related meetings
3. Daily deadline pressure
4. A discussion with the boss
5. Taking and making work-related phone calls

Friendships (14% of all daily stressors)
1. Argument with opposite sex (boyfriend or girl friend)
2. Waiting for a friend who is late
3. Anger over an interpersonal event
4. Arguments with friends
5. Socializing with a group of friends

Home responsibilities (10% of all daily stressors)
1. Doing housework (cooking, cleaning, etc) after a full day's work
2. Shopping (especially when crowded)
3. Machinery (heater, auto, etc.) not working
4. Short-run financial concerns

Traveling (9% of all daily stressors)
1. Riding the bus, train, or subway
2. Transportation delay on either side of a commute
3. Driving a car
4. Rushing to be somewhere on time
5. Being stuck in a traffic jam

Educational (7% of all daily stressors)
1. Being in class
2. Studying, reading, etc. (homework)
3. Taking a test
4. Asking questions in class
5. Teaching others in a class

Family (5% of all daily stressors)
1. Visiting relatives
2. Worrying about an offspring
3. Playing with and/or caring for an offspring after a day's work
4. Argument with your spouse
5. Scolding an offspring

Miscellaneous (8% of all daily stressors)
1. Insomnia for 30 minutes or less due to your thinking about the day's activities.
2. Going to the doctor or dentist
3. Being alone and feeling lonely

*"Daily Stressors," is taken from the *Book of Health,* copyright © 1981 by the American Health Foundation. It is used by permission of Franklin Watts, Inc.

THE SOCIAL READJUSTMENT RATING SCALE*

Score yourself on The Social Readjustment Rating Scale. What events have happened to you in the past 12 months?

Life Event

____	1. Death of spouse	100
____	2. Divorce	73
____	3. Marital separation from mate	65
____	4. Detention in jail or other institution	63
____	5. Death of a close family member	63
____	6. Major personal injury or illness	53
____	7. Marriage	50
____	8. Being fired at work	47
____	9. Marital reconciliation with mate	45
____	10. Retirement from work	45
____	11. Major change in the health or behavior of a family member	44
____	12. Pregnancy	40
____	13. Sexual difficulties	39
____	14. Gaining a new family member (e.g., through birth, adoption, oldster moving in, etc.)	39
____	15. Major business readjustment (e.g., merger, reorganization, bankruptcy, etc.)	39
____	16. Major change in financial state (e.g., a lot worse off or a lot better off than usual)	38
____	17. Death of a close friend	37
____	18. Change to a different line of work	36
____	19. Major change in number of arguments with spouse (e.g., either a lot more or a lot less than usual regarding child-rearing, personal habits, etc.)	35
____	20. Taking out a mortgage or a loan for a major purchase (e.g., for a home, business, etc.)	31
____	21. Foreclosure on a mortgage or a loan	30
____	22. Major change in responsibilities at work (e.g., promotion, demotion, lateral transfer)	29
____	23. Son or daughter leaving home (e.g., marriage,	

	attending college, etc.)	29
____	24. Trouble with in-laws	29
____	25. Outstanding personal achievement	28
____	26. Wife beginning or ceasing work outside the home	26
____	27. Beginning or ceasing formal schooling	26
____	28. Major change in living conditions (e.g., building a new home, remodeling, deterioration of home or neighborhood	25
____	29. Revision of personal habits (e.g., dress, manners, association, etc.)	24
____	30. Troubles with the boss	23
____	31. Major change in working hours or conditions	20
____	32. Change in residence	20
____	33. Changing to a new school	20
____	34. Major change in usual type and/or amount of recreation	19
____	35. Major change in church activities (e.g., a lot more or a lot less than usual)	19
____	36. Major change in social activities (e.g., clubs, dancing, movies, visiting, etc.)	18
____	37. Taking out a mortgage or loan for a lesser purchase (e.g., for a car, TV, freezer, etc.)	17
____	38. Major change in sleeping habits (e.g., a lot more or a lot less sleep, or change in part of day when asleep)	16
____	39. Major change in number of family get-togethers (e.g., a lot more or a lot less than usual)	15
____	40. Major change in eating habits (e.g., a lot more or a lot less food intake, or very different meal hours or surroundings)	15
____	41. Vacation	13
____	42. Christmas	12
____	43. Minor violations of the law (e.g., traffic tickets, jaywalking, disturbing the peace, etc.)	11

*From Holmes, T. H. and Rahe, R. H. "The Social Readjustment Rating Scale," Journal of *Psychosomatic Research 11* (1967): 213-218. Reprinted with permission from Pergamon Press, Ltd.

The helping professions cover a wide spectrum: doctors, lawyers, pastors, nurses, teachers, policemen, social workers, probation officers, psychologists, guidance counselors, mental health workers. The list goes on and on. The common denominator in all of these professions is people. They seek to help their fellowman with their particular service. We find burnout cutting across these occupational lines because of that common denominator.

THE HIGH COST OF HELPING PEOPLE

People's problems cause casualties among those who are trying to help. As many of us know, we have to pay a heavy price at times in order to have the privilege of helping others. Walter Alschuler, a clinical psychologist at the University of Massachusetts, gives this explanation: Burnout occurs in the helping professions "because human problems are not solvable in the same way that a problem with a car or a television set is solvable."[14]

A person often enters a helping profession initially because of a humanitarian motive. He wants to make the world, or at least the immediate community, a better place to live. For many, the size of the paycheck is a secondary consideration. The rewards sought are more than monetary; these persons want to see the quality of living improved for those they are serving. Of course, they assume their work will have many nonfinancial, emotional rewards, especially after they have been mislead by seeing or reading romanticized accounts of someone in their future profession. After years of training, they enter the working world with idealism and hope. It will not take them long to realize that there are times when they put more emotional energy into their helping work than they get back in the form of rewards. If the helper receives too many negative experiences and not enough positive rewards, this can easily contribute to burnout.[15]

Let us take, for example, a young pastor. He is told that his job is to add members to his church. He goes out with Bible in his hand to conquer the world. Many enter the ministry with the same misconception that I had: that people would fall in love with Christ, forsake their old ways of life, and embrace Christianity, if only they could be "enlightened" by a visit and a Bible study.

Soon, though, we discover that many reject Christianity; more people, in fact, than accept it. If a pastor cannot live with that fact, he will begin burning out early in his career. There have been times when I wished I could have pushed some "magic button" in a person which would make him do what is right. This, however, would have done away with his free will and the ministry of the Holy Spirit to convict him of truth.

A friend of mine is an occupational therapist at a school for the mentally retarded. He tells me that the stress level on his job is quite high because the tangible rewards seem to be few. In his own words, he says, "I teach these kids arts and crafts at the state school. For some of them, it is only a maintenance program. The majority of them will never get better; they will probably be institutionalized for life. I'll teach one of them a craft skill and he'll appear to be doing it quite well. But then he'll regress and forget the whole thing. What upsets me so much about my job is that I know so many of these kids are in our school as a result of physical and mental abuse by their parents. The stresses in my work caused me to quit a job in another state several years ago."

What happens when a helping professional burns out? He loses his ideals very often and begins working only for the paycheck. Usually the helper will seek to distance himself from his work and become as detached as possible. He will avoid contact with people. If all else fails, he will quit. The statistics about turnover in the helping professions are dramatic: 70 percent of nurses resign during any given year; 50 to 100 percent of child abuse/children protection workers resign.[16] The National Education Association reports that the average length of teacher service has dropped from 20 years to 14 years in the past 20 years.[17] Educators, particularly in the inner-city area, speak seriously of "teacher's combat neurosis."

THE EMPTY VOID

We can see, therefore, that those in the helping professions are very susceptible to the inroads of burnout. What can the helper do to protect himself? One important solution is discussed in the chapter "Turning Around a Bad Situation."

King Solomon had a problem. He tells us about it in Ecclesiastes. Early in his life he had given his heart to the Lord. When he ascended to Israel's throne, the Lord gladly fulfilled his request for wisdom and knowledge. He became the wisest man in the entire world. God also opened up the windows of heaven and poured out rich material blessings upon the king. Gradually, however, Solomon stopped praising and glorifying God. He turned inward, focusing the glory upon himself and his kingdom. He married numerous heathen wives—300 wives in all, besides 700 concubines. These women inevitably led his heart away from the God of heaven. Soon his apostasy was complete.

Solomon was still a very wise man, though, and he knew that something fundamental was missing in his life. He was like the jigsaw puzzle with one piece missing, and he began searching vigorously for that missing piece. In Ecclesiastes he describes his quest for inner happiness and for the meaning of life. He started by pursuing intellectual matters, but this left him unfulfilled. "I told myself, 'I have become a great man, far wiser than anyone who ruled Jerusalem before me. I know what wisdom and knowledge really are.' I was determined to learn the difference between knowledge and foolishness, wisdom and madness. But I found that I might as well be chasing the wind." Ecclesiastes 1:16, 17, TEV. He then sought to find lasting meaning in the pleasures the world offered. "I decided to enjoy myself and find out what happiness is. But I found that this is useless, too. I discovered that laughter is foolish, that pleasure does you no good." Chapter 2, verses 1, 2, TEV. Realizing the emptiness found in this, he turned to materialism. "I accomplished great things. I built myself houses and planted vineyards. I planted gardens and orchards, with all kinds of fruit trees in them. . . . I also piled up silver and gold from the royal treasuries of the lands I ruled. Men and women sang to entertain me, and I had all the women a man could want." Verses 4-8, TEV. So we find Solomon trying to find happiness through money and possessions, musical entertainment, and sexual gratification. This story happened around 3000 years ago, but it reads like the lives of many individuals today.

Solomon surveys all that he had with apparent satisfaction, but then he states his true feelings: "Anything I wanted, I got. I did not deny myself any pleasure. I was proud of everything I had worked for, and all this was my reward. Then I thought about all that I had done and how hard I had worked doing it, and I realized that it didn't mean a thing. It was like chasing the wind—of no use at all." Verses 10, 11, TEV. Finally Solomon declares in utter frustration, "So life came to mean nothing to me." The King James Version reads, "Therefore, I hated life." Does this sound familiar? Have you ever heard a friend or loved one tell you that they hate what life has brought to them and that they wish they could cease living altogether? If they tell you this, it is likely they have had an experience similar to Solomon's. King Solomon, in his alienation from his heavenly Father, was experiencing what we would call today "a severe burnout." It was only in his later years that he was able to see life from a realistic and clear viewpoint; only then did he find lasting peace and happiness.

After years of traveling down dead-end pathways, a sadder but wiser Solomon concludes his book with this appeal: "Remember now thy Creator in the days of thy youth, while the evil days come not, nor the years draw nigh, when thou shalt say, I have no pleasure in them." Then he says, "Let us hear the conclusion of the whole matter: Fear God, and keep his commandments: for this is the whole duty of man." Ecclesiastes 12:1, 13.

The experience of Solomon shows us that there will always be an aching need within our beings if we fail to develop a living connection with the Lord. We need His Spirit at work in our lives to comfort and guide us. Karl Barth in his writings calls that need inside of us "the God-shaped vacuum." We might try to fill up that vacuum with anything and everything under the sun: music, television, human friends, clothes, intellectual pursuits, water skiing, home improvements, cars, video games, Sunday-afternoon and Monday-night football, the accumulation of money, even our jobs. We can fill up the void in life with "things," even good things, but the soul will continue hungering for Someone much greater than you or I.

Could it be that the modern burnout phenomenon is, at its most basic level, society's statement of spiritual bankruptcy? The psychologist or sociologist from a humanistic background would contend that this is not the case. Most likely he would deny the existence of God, together with the fact that man has a spiritual nature. These facts, though, cannot be denied if one honestly studies the evidence. Dr. Herbert J. Freudenberger, a leading burnout researcher, does not profess to be a Christian. But interestingly enough he points out in his book where the roots of burnout can be found: "A big reason our lives are more difficult today and more prone to burnout is our repudiation of religion and the buffers it provides for dealing with uncomfortable issues and situations. Because we no longer accept explanations of faith and have not formulated satisfactory communal substitutes, we have to improvise our own solutions to every problem that comes along, even the trivial disappointments of daily living. This is not only difficult, it's also confusing and burdensome."[18]

If we turn our backs upon God and no longer place our faith in Him, we have no real help in time of need; there is no "balm in Gilead." The familiar hymn tells us, "O what peace we often forfeit, O what needless pain we bear, all because we do not carry everything to God in prayer." If modern man seeks to do away with God, he also does away with all moral absolutes by which to direct his life. He becomes like a giant ship with no rudder drifting on the sea. The will of God is replaced with a do-it-yourself lifestyle. Like the people of ancient Israel during the judges, we do what is right in our own eyes. The Gestalt credo of Frederick Perls declares, "I do my thing, and you do your thing. . . . You are You and I am I. And if by chance we find each other, it's beautiful; if not, it can't be helped."[19] But is this the way we really want to live? Burnout has a definite spiritual dimension. For that reason, a spiritual solution is imperative. We cannot merely apply psychological Band-Aids to cover up deep spiritual wounds. We need the touch of the Healer, and we will learn how to do so in the final chapter of this book.

Burnout makes its impact upon our lives as a result of its three major contributors: (1) stress (2) the human problems one faces as a professional helper (3) unmet spiritual needs. Now that we have a clearer picture of what burnout is and what brings it about, we are now ready to examine some practical suggestions concerning how to counteract its effects upon our lives. But first, take a look at you as a worker and the place where you work. Ask yourself this important question, "Is Your Work Making You Sick?"

1. Notes of Burnout Workshop conducted at St. Anthony's Hospital, Oklahoma City, Oklahoma, March 1982.

2. Randall Schuler, "The Invisible Disease May Be Killing You," *Your Life and Health*, February 1982.

3. Hans Selye, *Stress Without Distress* (New York: New American Library, 1974), p. 14

4. Hans Selye quoted in Dave Schwantes, "Stress for Success" Walla Walla College *Alumni Review*, Summer 1979.

5. Hans Selye, *The Stress of Life* (New York: McGraw-Hill, 1956), p. viii.

6. Rosalind Forbes, *Corporate Stress* (Garden City, New York: Doubleday, 1979), p. 173-193.

7. *Ibid.*, chapter on "Stressful Occupations."

8. Betty LeVoy, "Noise Pollution Causes Additional Stress," *Lifestyles*, vol. 1, no. 4.

9. *Ibid.*

10. Jonathan Freedman, *Crowding and Behavior* (New York: Viking Press, 1979), pp. 23, 25.

11. *Ibid.*, p. 57.

12. Gary Collins, *You Can Profit From Stress* (Santa Ana, Calif: Vision House, 1977,), pp. 27-29, and Ernest L. Wynder, ed. *The Book of Health* (New York: Watts, 1981), p. 387.

13. Wynder, p. 387.

14. *The Sunday Oklahoman*, 5 April 1981.

15. Notes from Burnout Workshop.

16. *Ibid.*

17. *The Sunday Oklahoman*, 5 April 1981.

18. Herbert J. Freudenberger with Geraldine Richelson, *Burnout: How to Beat the High Cost of Success* (New York: Bantam Books, 1981), p. 88.

19. Quoted in *Bartlett's Familiar Quotations*, John Bartlett, ed. (Boston: Little Brown, and Co, 1980).

Is Your Work Making You Sick?

"I'd rather wear out than rust out," remarked James White, an early pioneer in the Adventist Church.

Imagine what an emotional and physical strain you would be under if God had asked you to be one of the human founders of a great religious movement. Think of the hard work needed to establish institutions and churches. Think also of the sleepless nights to be spent in writing articles for periodicals and digging out truths of the Bible in long study sessions with fellow believers. If you can identify with the burden of people's souls and the urgency of the message of the return of Jesus, then you can sympathize with men like James White and J. N. Andrews. They were early Seventh-day Adventists who both overworked in God's cause and consequently went to an early grave.

Their dedication was unquestioned. Young John Andrews at the age of twenty-three wrote these courageous words in the *Review and Herald*, November 25, 1851: "In the midst of tribulation and affliction, my soul is joyful in God. I was never more deeply impressed with the importance of the work in which we are engaged, than at the present time. My heart is bound up in it, and in a work so sacred I would cheerfully spend and be spent. Souls are perishing, who may now be reached, the time for labor is short, the night in which no man can work is at hand." This was still his attitude in 1874 as he went to serve in Europe as an overseas missionary for the newly organized Seventh-day Adventist denomination. There he spent his time establishing new periodicals, writing, evangelizing and teaching the people in various places. He knew his health was declining as he labored in Europe, but he did not slow his pace. He worked on and on, even when he contracted tuberculosis. He gave every remaining ounce of his strength to the cause of God until the day of his death in 1883. He died in the prime of life, at the age of fifty-four.[1]

Many of you have seen the picture of James White, carrying the first edition of *The Present Truth* in a carpetbag to Middletown, Connecticut, eight miles from his home. This act is symbolic of the dedicated spirit of him and his wife Ellen. At times they were so poor that they had to decide between buying food or clothing for their babies. Still, they gave themselves unreservedly to the Advent movement. In those early years, James mowed hay, hauled stone, or did other jobs so that an issue of his paper could be published. He did this hard manual labor with a constant, sharp pain in his side.

As the work grew and became organized, James White's commitment to it did not weaken. Every task which he undertook was done with great spirit and vigor. He was a natural leader, and this quality always placed him at the forefront of the new church organization. At one time or another, he was editor and/or publisher of the *Review and Herald, Youth's Instructor, Signs of the Times*, and the *Health Reformer*; president of the General Conference; and chairman of the board at Battle Creek College.

James and Ellen White attended and spoke at camp meetings all over the nation; they worked together in founding institutions. While his leadership ability was much needed, he ultimately suffered greatly because he labored too hard and allowed himself to be weighted down with too many heavy burdens and cares. Personal attacks against him also had their toll. He suffered feebleness of health, especially from the early 1860s until his death. His first stroke came in 1865.

During this period, many other leaders in the church fell victim to serious illnesses. Arthur Spalding writes: "For nearly a year no quorum of either the General Conference Committee or the Michigan Conference committee could be had, because of the illness of a majority."[2]

Following James White's paralyzing stroke of 1865, he was unable to lead in the church for a year and a half. When he recuperated, he tried again to resume the burdens which he had carried before. But in 1871 he had another stroke, and another in 1877. He died in 1881 at the age of sixty, after a very brief illness.

These two brief illustrations, that of the life of J. N. Andrews and of James White, were not given to criticize these dedicated early Advent pioneers. Instead, their experience helps us to understand more clearly the counsels and warnings which Ellen G. White gave to the Adventist Church about the dangers of overwork in any line of endeavor.

"We should practice temperance in our labor. It is not our duty to place ourselves where we shall be overworked. Some may at times be placed where this is necessary, but it should be the exception, not the rule. We are to practice temperance in all things. If we honor the Lord by acting our part, He will on His part preserve our health. . . .

"As a rule, the labor of the day should not be prolonged into the evening. . . . I have been shown that those who do this often lose much more than they gain, for their energies are exhausted, and they labor on nervous excitement. They may not realize any immediate injury, but they are surely undermining their constitution."[3]

"There is a need that God's chosen workmen should listen to the command to go apart and rest awhile. Many valuable lives have been sacrificed because of a disregard of this command. . . . When nature uttered a protest, they paid no heed, but did double the work they should have done; and God laid them in the grave to rest until the last trump shall sound to call the righteous forth to immortality."[4]

WORK OVERLOAD

The problem of work overload remains a chronic one in today's world, a hundred years after those words were written. It plagues even those engaged in seemingly ordinary occupations, those who are not leading out in the founding of a religious movement or any other great cause. Certainly overwork is perceived to be a much greater problem today, due to the ever-quickening pace of our lives. *Psychology Today* recently conducted a study in which they surveyed the attitudes of workers. Three fourths of those surveyed complained about having to take their work, troubles, and frustrations home with them from the job. Every person interviewed said their work was "basically rewarding," but they resented their work when it cut into their leisure or family time. One fourth felt they worked excessively long hours, having to go to work too early and leave too late. One fifth said they were finding it "extremely difficult" to complete work assignments in the allotted time. One fifth also said that their work schedules generally interfered with their family life.[5]

The English critic, John Ruskin, once wrote: "In order for people to be happy in their work, these three things are needed: They must be fit for it; they must not have too much of it; and they must have a sense of success in it." The first prerequisite for the happy worker is that he must be physically fit. If he is not in good health, even the most routine of tasks may seem like a crushing weight to him. Success is also needed. Too many negative experiences without any successes is the quickest path there is to burnout. "They must not have too much of it." The overloaded worker can be burdened down in two ways. There is *qualitative overload*: "the job assignment demands more extensive skills, abilities and knowledge than the person has." *Quantitative overload* also exists, where the worker simply has too much to do within the allotted time on the job.[6] Both of these overload conditions lead to stress, which in turn blossoms into the worker's burnout.

Says Dr. Ray Rosenman, a noted cardiologist: "The greatest stress is the one that keeps an individual constantly feeling impatient, constantly hurrying and giving him the feeling that he has not done everything he feels he should have done in a single working day."[7] As the chart in the last chapter shows, work-related stress accounts for 47 percent of all the stress most of us encounter each day. If this is true, then it follows that we all should take a closer look at the different elements of our job which make us feel stressful and how we are relating to those elements. Failing to do this might, in the end, cause us to sacrifice our health.

The way we relate to the work environment is a highly individual matter. People go to work each morning with many different attitudes. Some persons are not motivated to accomplish very much on their job. They float through life with no worries about accomplishment, so they never disappoint themselves. As someone commented a few years ago: "When we get enough money to live for a couple of weeks, unless we're doing something creative, we'll probably stop work. It's not because we're lazy, but because we think there are far more valuable things to do with our lives. We think that to waste life doing repetitive jobs is blasphemy."[8]

Some people perform in "spurts": their pendulum swings between enthusiasm and apathy, between vigorous activity and loafing. Then there are the workaholics of society, the highly motivated ones who push ahead with ambitious projects and who thrive on pressures and deadlines. Most of us are somewhere in between. We have the motivation to do a good job, we work diligently, but we resist too heavy of a work load. I believe this is the healthiest approach of all. Within each one of us is a small voice which warns us to stay away from work overload. Some of us listen to that voice; others ignore it. Those of us who ignore it often find ourselves struggling under the heavy burden of overwork.

This work overload can even be self-inflicted; one's boss and peers may be pleased with one's work output while the individual is not. He is in constant competition with himself. Laboring under feelings of inferiority, the employee thinks he has not done enough and therefore pushes on to accomplish more and more. Such a person may grow bitter and hostile at his superiors, while he only has himself to blame.

WORKAHOLICS

While we are taking a look at the different types of workers and how they relate to work and work overload, it would be good for us to take a closer look at that group known as "workaholics." Marilyn Machlowitz gives an in-depth profile of them in her book *Workaholics—Living With Them, Working With Them*. She describes a workaholic as someone who loves his work but also is addicted to it. He finds it quite difficult to relax and do nothing; vacations bore him. Instead, this type of person would rather be at his desk working, preferably for long periods of time. While the worker described above despises the work overload dumped upon him, the workaholic invites an overload of work. It doesn't bother him. Other people work in order to make a living, but a workaholic lives so that he might work. His work is his reason for existence, his constant obsession. One illustration from her book points this out: "Even New York City's 1977 blackout couldn't keep workaholics at home. Several hundreds of people went to work despite the knowldge that buildings would be locked and businesses closed. I found them pacing impatiently outside their offices, demanding to be allowed to enter, even if reaching their desks would require climbing thirty flights of stairs. Others went about their business on the street."[9]

Instead of being an angry, burdened-down person, the workaholic appears to be quite happy and contented. He will gladly work twelve and fourteen hours a day, seven days a week on an ongoing basis; he will not complain at all. You may ask, "What's wrong with that? Let him work compulsively, if that brings him pleasure." There is a problem with that solution, however. While he may give the appearance of being happy and contented, the workaholic has an imbalanced life. One aspect of life—his work—completely dominates. This personality syndrome causes havoc with marriages and the parent-child relationship. He is married to his job rather than to his wife; he becomes the invisible father. Also, his manner of working causes great stress among those he works with. He may expect his colleagues to work in exactly the same manner as he does, and becomes irritated when they do not. The pressure-cooker atmosphere they create causes fellow workers to burn out, according to Machlowitz. And despite their supposed limitless supply of energy, the workaholic himself is far from immune to the burnout phenomenon.[10]

The religion of Christ promotes a balanced, restful life-style. Although the work ethic is pronounced in the Scriptures, we are told there is something even more important: "Labour not for the meat which perisheth, but for that meat which endureth unto everlasting life.'' John 6:27. We are told in the fourth command-ment, ''Six days shalt thou labour, and do all thy work: but the seventh day is the sabbath of the Lord thy God: in it thou shalt not do any work.'' Part of this command tells us that it is God's will that we work for six days during the week; to spend them in laziness would be contrary to His plan for us. However, He calls us apart on the seventh day for our spiritual, mental, and physical renewal. This day helps fulfill the command Christ once gave to His disciples: ''Come ye yourselves apart into a desert place, and rest a while.'' Mark 6:31.

Is your job making you sick? Or stated in the more positive manner, is your job allowing you to stay well and happy? It would be helpful at this point for you to take the ''Wellness at Work Inventory.'' This instrument, developed by an organization called Life/Work Management, measures how ones occupation or profession is contributing to one's overall well-being as a person. It shows numerous factors encountered during the working hours which contribute to that well-being.

Your final score will be on a scale of 1 to 10, depending upon your response to the following 26 statements.

WELLNESS AT WORK INVENTORY

This test is taken from Life Work Management. Assign a score of 1 to 10 to each statement. Total your score and divide by 26 to find your average score per question.

_____ a. I thoroughly enjoy using the skills my work demands.

_____ b. I am living in my favorite geographical environment.

_____ c. I do my work because I want to do it and because I enjoy doing it—not because I ''have to pay the bills.''

_____ d. I am pleased with the distance I commute to work.

_____ e. At work I use special knowledge or training that I enjoy.

_____ f. I work with people (colleagues, clients, supervisors, subordinates) I like.

_____ g. I am comfortable in my work.

_____ h. I am confident in my work.

_____ i. I am creative in my work.

_____ j. My work expresses my meaning and purpose in life.

_____ k. My work is important and valuable to society.

_____ l. I enjoy the physical setting of my work.

_____ m. I like the conditions under which I work (time schedules, policies, work place, and pacing.)

_____ n. My work is easy and yet sufficiently challenging for me.

_____ o. There is no other activity than my present work that I would rather do for pay.

_____ p. There is nothing I do for play that I would rather be doing as work for pay.

_____ q. I am paid sufficiently for my work.

_____ r. My work mixes well with the type and frequency of relationships I like (family friends, colleagues).

_____ s. My way of working leaves me sufficient time for unstructured, noncompetitive leisure.

_____ t. My way of working leaves me sufficient resources for pursuing my other interests, favorite hobbies, and educational goals.

_____ u. I am working at the supervisory level I want.

_____ v. I am working with the number and kind of people I like.

_____ w. I do my work as an expression of being who-I-am, rather than as an attempt to become who-I-could-be or as an effort to get or buy something (early retirement, house, vacation, benefits).

_____ x. I feel great energy when doing my work.

_____ y. I am fully myself (dress, emotional expressiveness, truthfulness) at work.

_____ z. I can change jobs/careers any time I choose.

Eugene E. Jennings, Ph.D. professor of management, Graduate School of Business, Michigan State University, East Lansing, says, ''I find that burnout doesn't occur just because of boredom and fatigue at work. The spectrum of the person's whole life is out of shape. Granted, it may have started at work, but no other part of that person's life is regenerating him enough so that he can put up with the boredom and fatigue at work. And when that happens, you've got a true case of burnout.

"If this description applies to you, you should take a good look at your whole life-style, your values and goals. Otherwise, you're going to find that you're trying to do something about one end of your life while the other end is still dangling."[11]

1. Arthur W. Spalding, *Origin and History of Seventh-day Adventists* (Washington, D.C.: Review and Herald Publishing Assn., 1961), vol. 1, p. 209.

2. *Ibid*, p. 355.

3. Ellen G. White, *Child Guidance* (Nashville, Tenn.: Southern Publishing Assn., 1954), p. 397.

4. Ellen G. White, *Gospel Workers* (Washington, D.C.: Review and Herald Publishing Assn., 1915), p. 245.

5. Patricia Renwick and Edward Lawler, "What You Really Want From Your Job," *Psychology Today*, May 1978, pp. 53-65.

6. Rosalind Forbes, *Corporate Stress* (Garden City, New York: Doubleday, 1974), p. 36.

7. *Ibid.*, p. 79.

8. "Dropouts With a Mission," *Newsweek*, 6 February 1967, p. 95.

9. Marilyn Machlowitz, *Workaholics: Living With Them, Working With Them* (New York: New American Library, 1980), p. 4.

10. *Ibid*, pp. 51, 159.

11. Quoted in Seymour Shubin, "Burnout: The Professional Hazard You Face in Nursing," Nursing 78, 8(1978):27.

These "Cures" Won't Help You

When a person begins to burn out, he develops an approach to living which can best be described as numb and listless. It is a state of mind which even the victim cannot understand, but he knows that he must do something to lessen the pain. So the victim often begins grasping at straws; he will do anything to feel alive and happy again.

False cures for burnout come in many varieties. Our society is especially fond of turning to chemical solutions when the going gets rough—alcohol, marijuana, LSD, cocaine, and prescription pills. This tendency in a large degree stems from the popular hedonistic notion that our lives should be characterized by a perpetual high and that we should never experience any emotional distress or the "valleys" of life. Some think it is asking too much to have to face reality. So they decide to enter the realm of "non-reason." They believe non-rationality will give to their lives the meaning which they missed in the straight world. (This concept of "non-reason" is explained in depth in the writings of Francis Shaeffer, especially in *How Should We Then Live?*) "Reality hurts—therefore, I will escape it" is the attitude of millions. The only hitch is that the same problems are there staring them in the face when they come down from their drug-induced high.

DRUGS—NO CURE
The deceptive nature of drug and alcohol use is spelled out by Mike Warnke, Christian speaker/humorist, in his own distinctive style: "You get two weeks behind on your rent, so you decide,

54

'Well, I'm behind on my rent; guess I'll get high. Maybe it will go away.' So you get strung out on dope and stay that way for two weeks. When you come down, you are now four weeks behind on your rent. When you got high you didn't have any food in the icebox. When you come back down you find out that somebody has stolen your icebox.

"It's a progressive deal—it just gets worse and worse. The only thing that dope does for you is to cloud your vision so that you can't see that things are getting worse and worse. By the time you come to your senses, you are in up to your neck. Drugs are really a trap, man. It's one of the worst traps you can get yourself into."[1]

If you've ever heard one of Warnke's records or tapes, you know that he speaks from experience.

OTHER CAMOUFLAGES

People use many other kinds of devices to camouflage their burnout and give their daily existence a sense of aliveness. They may become hooked on horse and casino gambling, or perhaps on pornography because these activities are outwardly exciting. They somehow do not realize the moral and psychological damage these activities cause until it is too late. They may become involved in dangerous sports such as stock car racing and sky diving in hopes of alleviating their numbed state. Ideally, they are able to get away from these sports with their bodies still intact, but their burnout remains.

We've all heard of the frustrated middle-aged male who suddenly runs away from his wife and family, gets a sports car and a new wardrobe, adopts a youthful hairstyle, and begins dating his twenty-one-year-old secretary. This so-called "mid-life crisis" occurs because this man has been suffering from the symptoms of burnout for months or even years, but he has not done anything positive to counteract it. Finally, he arrives at the place where his emptiness catches up with him. He feels the only way to invest his life with any meaning is to go wild for a while and rebel against every principle which has guided his life in the past. Instead of improving his life, however, such a course only leads to further unhappiness and eventual destruction of mind, body, and soul.

Some individuals may employ methods which do not seem so drastic and foolish. They perhaps will use an added workload to mask the pain which burnout brings to them. Twelve-hour workdays become common. Such persons are submerging themselves deeper and deeper into the very activities which caused them to arrive at their present state. In addition, large numbers of people today escape through the entertainment medium—television, theater-going, recorded music, concerts.

Whatever the particular crutch the burnout victim is using, the following principle holds true: "Where burnout exists, the sufferer unwittingly selects a cure which intensifies the burnout, spreading it faster and faster."[2]

Are you relying upon certain distractions and forms of escape in order to make you feel better? If so, make a list of such items. Notice how often during the day your mind is occupied with them and how much you talk about them. It could be that what you have listed are legitimate, helpful diversions which you need to be able to cope with life. On the other hand, you may pinpoint a false cure which you have been using to camouflage and cover up an aching need within. If this is the case, then do not use them any longer. Realize that the false cures will not bring you any good results, but ultimately they will bring you much harm. What you need is a real and lasting solution.

1. Mike Warnke, *Mike Warnke Alive* (phonograph album) Word Incorporated, 1976.

2. Herbert J. Freudenberger with Geraldine Richelson, *Burnout: How to Beat the High Cost of Success*, (New York: Bantam Books, 1981), p. 104.

Turning Around a Bad Situation

View your burnout as a crossroads experience. If nothing is done about your present state of mind, you certainly will slide down into a more serious, perhaps life-threatening condition. It has been said that the only difference between being in a rut and being in the grave is the dimensions of the hole you are in. On the other hand, if you are able to pull out of the burned-out state into a higher, more satisfying way of life, your overall experience probably will be more fulfilling than if you had never burned out at all. If burnout is the equivalent of ''running on empty,'' then realize that your attempts to pull out of it are like a refueling pit stop. This is not the end of the road for you, just a necessary detour.

It took months, maybe even years, to get into the state you find yourself in today. Therefore, do not expect to be fully recovered in two weeks. That would be unrealistic. Patience is the virtue you must cultivate during this time—patience with yourself and patience with others. You may not realize progress as fast you would like, and that can be frustrating. However, do not lose hope. If you do, then you'll find yourself sliding back to where you are right now.

A STRATEGY FOR SURVIVAL

In order for you to pull out of the burned-out state, you must formulate a coping strategy. In other words, you must ask yourself, ''What are the things I should do to get from where I am now to where I would like to be?'' Preferably, your strategy should be put in writing. Also, it must be a personalized one; the strategy I have developed for myself might be irrelevant for your situation.

When you develop this strategy or "game plan" to counteract burnout, you have won almost half the battle. You have pinpointed the specifics of the problem and developed an intelligent solution to it. But the greater part of the battle is actually implementing the strategy in day-to-day living. That can be pretty tough. After a while, the natural tendency will be to treat your burnout strategy like glorified New Year's resolutions and to not really take them seriously. (That will be especially true once you begin to see some progress in your condition.) But don't do that, because your burnout stratgy is really a strategy for survival.

In the next few pages are listed twenty steps which are useful in escaping burnout. Some of them, like the last one, "Communion and fellowship with the Lord," apply to everyone. Other steps will not apply to you. Maybe an important coping tool has not been included in this list, although I've tried to cover all the bases. If this is true, then the sudden flash of insight which you may receive while mowing the lawn or doing the laundry might just be what you need! Further insights can be gleaned from the books listed at the end of the book.

TWENTY STEPS IN ESCAPING BURNOUT

1. *Review your philosophy of life.* Ask yourself, What are the things in my life which I consider to be the most important? Is getting ahead professionally the supreme object of life, or do I have my profession in its proper place? Take a look at where your religious experience is. Is it something which you confine to two hours a week, or does it have top priority every day? How important are human relationships to you—your family and friends—in comparison with your work? Take stock of the four main areas of your life: the physical, mental, spiritual, and social. How badly are they out of balance due to your burned-out condition?

Look into the future. Establish for yourself some long-term and short-term objectives. Part of the problem you face may be due to the fact that you do not have any closely defined direction to your life. You keep pushing ahead, day by day, week by week, but you do not have a view of the big picture.

2. *Be aware that you are going through a major crisis in your life. Do not seek to deceive yourself into thinking that all is well, when in fact you are hurting inside.*

Many people are too proud to acknowledge the fact that they have anything lacking within themselves. Being true Laodiceans, they firmly declare about their lives, "I am rich, and increased with goods, and have need of nothing." Denial is always damaging to a person, because it only postpones the inevitable: the need to take a good, honest look at himself and his situation. It is even possible to submerge oneself into a round of never-ending "good" activities in order to avoid the needed soul-searching. The old saying certainly applies here: "You can run, but you can't hide." Burnout and its symptoms will eventually catch up with you, of this you can be sure.

Awareness, the exact opposite of denial, is an essential component in recovering from burnout. Awareness means that you simply take a good, honest look at yourself and your situation. By becoming aware, you refuse to rationalize away your condition by saying, "Well, that's life. I can't expect anything better for myself." You realize life has more to offer than what you're currently experiencing.[2]

Increasing your awareness does not mean that you turn yourself into an emotional hypochondriac. You do not need constantly to run around and tell everyone how you feel. Awareness is primarily for *your* benefit, and much of it should be self-contained. However, you should turn to certain key individuals for help and guidance during this difficult time. (See section 6 about support systems.)

3. *Analyze which life events are causing you to feel stressful and burned out. Having done that, think of how you will relate to those events and situations in the future.*

Remember this: the cause of your burnout cannot be placed solely at your doorstep. You have not arrived here only because of a character weakness or inadequacy which you might possess. There are stress factors in your work and home environment which have precipitated the burnout. Of course, these stressful things may be bothering others around you too. This is one of the reasons why support groups are important. (While you are delaying with these stress factors, make sure that none of them are your own fault. We punish ourselves at times with stressful situations of our own creation, then we blame those around us for our self-inflicted anxiety.)

In her book *Burnout: From Tedium to Personal Growth*, Dr. Ayala Pines describes the four major coping strategies for stress:

Direct Active

You can change the source of the stress (such as, transferring to a new department).

You can confront the source.

You can adopt a positive attitude about it.

Indirect Active

You can talk about the source of the stress.

You can change something about yourself.

You can get involved in other activities.

Direct-Inactive

You can ignore the source of the stress.

You can avoid that source.

You can leave from the presence of the source.

Indirect-Inactive (not recommended because it weakens the individual rather than helping him)

You can become involved in alcohol and drugs.

You can become ill and collapse because of the stress.

You can worry and cry about the stress.[3]

Direct action is defined as a strategy which is applied externally to the source itself. Indirect action involves a strategy applied internally to one's behavior. Dr. Pines says there exists also an active-inactive dimension in dealing with this problem. An active coping strategy would confront the source of the stress, while an inactive coping strategy would withdraw from it.

From the first three groupings, a person must decide which solution is best for his or her situation. There are times, for example, when it is important to confront someone at work who is causing you stress and anxiety. At other times, it would be wiser and safer to ignore and avoid that source, or even, if possible, to develop a positive attitude about him (even if he is impossible to work with!). The worst response that someone can have to a stressful situation is denying that it exists. We need to honestly and wisely deal with the problems that come our way. If we don't, then they will only grow larger. Please notice that a distinction is made between *avoidance* and *ignoring* on the one hand, and *denial* on the other. Those who choose to avoid and ignore still realize a problem exists, but they have decided not to confront the stress source head on.[4]

4. *Consider changing parts of your life which bring you chronic stress.*

No, I'm not saying you should divorce your husband or wife. They may be causing you a tremendous amount of stress, but separation, and especially divorce, should be thought of as last resorts. (Isn't it curious that many divorced people marry again, with their second marriage often having the same tension, stress, and unhappiness as their first one did?) Major and minor *adjustments* are needed from time to time in a marriage in order to keep it healthy. As the two marital partners communicate with one another, they accomplish the task of adjusting to each other's minds and expectations. If they fail to make these adjustments throughout their marriage, then the problems get worse. Eventually, they reach the conclusion that a major *change* is needed—namely, separation and divorce. How often a little mid-course correction would keep a marriage from ending up on the rocks!

When I use the word *change*, I am referring to the times when you leave your present pursuits and goals, choosing to walk away from them entirely and begin again. At times this change is needed, especially in the work and study environment. Change is needed when you find yourself trying to do tasks which are totally beyond your abilities. This imbalance naturally makes a person uptight and tense.[5] For example, a salesman may feel his monthly quotas are too much of a burden, and he does not consider the pressure worth it. Perhaps you may find yourself in a position which requires giving a lot of orders and directions, but you feel very uncomfortable doing so. If you are a follower, rather than a leader, then you should be functioning in the role of a follower, not a leader.

A good friend I'll call Jim illustrates what happens when someone gets involved in an endeavor which he or she is not physically, mentally, or emotionally able to bear. Jim's experience shows how burnout can end in tragedy. Jim decided he wanted to become a medical doctor. So he gained admission into the large medical school near my home. As far as intellectual ability was concerned, Jim had what it takes. He was a very intelligent young man, as evidenced by the fine lessons and sermons he presented in my church. However, he was unable to cope with certain aspects of the program at the medical school—the competition for grades, the long hours of study, and strained relationships with several of the professors.

All of this was too much for Jim, and he suffered his first nervous breakdown about two years after entering medical school. He dropped out for a while, and he seemed to be doing much better. But his obsession to be a doctor caught up with him, and he reentered his course of study. Six months later, he was back in the psychiatric ward with another nervous breakdown. He left the medical school for good and moved back to his hometown. Unfortunately, he could never get over the fact that he had dropped out of medical school. Jim ended his life with a gunshot to the head.

How much better if only he had matched his life's work with his emotional and physical abilities! He wanted to help people and to restore their health. Perhaps he could have become a nurse, a medical technologist, or a physician's assistant and would have enjoyed that work. Most important, he would have been able to handle it, while at the same time fulfilling, to a certain degree, his ambition to have a career in the healing profession. Any career change or detour (whatever it is) is preferable to a series of nervous breakdowns and eventual suicide.

5. *Learn to accept what you cannot change about your life and work.*

Situations arise, such as in Jim's case, where a job or even a career change is necessary to escape burnout. On the other hand, it is not necessary to "jump ship" every time something goes wrong in one's life and work. Often what is needed is a "breaking in" period. During this span of time you should seek to come to grips with the difficult situation you are facing. If you are new on the job, for example, do not quit when the going gets rough. If possible, try to stay long enough to learn how to perform that job. You may then discover that the job is just not for you, and then you may want to consider a change.

Someone has penned the "Serenity Prayer." You probably saw it in this book's flyleaf. It is such a wise prayer that I'd like to repeat it in a popularized version. "God, grant me the serenity to accept the things I cannot change, courage to change the things I can, and the wisdom to know the difference." Certain situations are incapable of being changed. Others can be changed, although it might take considerable effort. (At times the struggle to bring about the change may not really be worth it.)

Psychologists have a term for the *wisdom* of knowing what one can change and what one cannot change; they call it "cognitive clarity." Their study has shown that this cognitive clarity is one of the important steps one must take in order to pull out of the burnout state. Says Dr. Pines: "Burnout often manifests itself in people who assume that everything destructive and dehumanizing can be changed. These people invariably end up banging their heads against the stone wall of a nonresponsive bureaucracy. Some aspects of a bureaucracy simply cannot be changed. After trying and failing, they obviously begin feeling helpless and hopeless and come to believe that *nothing* can be changed."[6] Cognitive clarity protects us from falling into such a trap.

What do you do when you are faced with a situation which is unchangeable and far from ideal? Do you grit your teeth and block out the unpleasantness from your mind? Occasionally you have to do this. A better state of mind in which to find yourself, however, is a state of contentment. Paul the apostle knew a lot about unpleasant life experiences. He was stoned, shipwrecked, imprisoned, and ridiculed for the sake of the gospel. But here is what he says about his inner contentment. "I am saying this because I am in need, for I have learned to be content whatever the circumstances. I know what it is to be in need, and I know what it is to have plenty. I have learned the secret of being content in any and every situation, whether well fed or hungry, whether living in plenty or in want. I can do everything through him who gives me strength." Philippians 4:11-13, NIV. Life may not have been much fun for the apostle Paul at times, but he found continual contentment through being "in Christ." His happiness and contentment was not dependent upon circumstances, because he lived above them.

6. *Talk out your problems and frustrations; establish a support system with those around you.*

You and I are all social creatures and therefore are in need of one another for sympathy, encouragement, advice, and self-improvement. You cannot shut yourselves up in isolation and then expect to have a fulfilling existence. A large part of your meaning in life is derived from human relationships. Emotional well-being and stability is also dependent upon the healthy interaction with others.

Perhaps the most important social system to which you belong is the family. It is from the family that you learned so much about life in your early years. Most adults also belong to a family in which they have a spouse and children. You should be able to expect much love and support from your family if it is based upon sound, Christian principles. In addition, you form a network of friends throughout your life. Some of these friendship bonds are long-term, while others last only a few months, or at the most a couple of years. Often the bond of friendship established with others evaporates when one moves to a different locale. For the Christian, the church provides a quality of fellowship and friendship which is difficult for others to understand. The church is a special family—the family of God. It is, or should be, a caring community of love and support. Along with all of the above, social systems of support are formed among those one works with. These include relationships with supervisors, subordinates, colleagues, and clients.

If the relationships with those with whom you work, play, worship, and live with are not satisfactory, then you will have a greater tendency to burn out and find life to be miserable. By the same token, a caring group or network of individuals can be of invaluable help to someone who has been experiencing symptoms of burnout.[7] Help from other people is a coping strategy which is often overlooked, mainly because one is naturally reluctant to expose his or her weaknesses and inadequacies to others. They do not want to appear vulnerable. However, they rob themselves of much help in life because of this attitude.

Social support systems have been defined by Gerald Caplan as "enduring interpersonal ties to groups of people who can be relied upon to provide emotional sustenance, assistance, and resources in times of need, who provide feedback, and who share standards and values." They are "the people who support an individual through crises and calm and with whom feelings can be shared without condemnation."[8]

Several important functions can be accomplished by the different people who operate as one's social support group. These functions are as follows:

Listening. You need those who are willing to listen with sympathy and understanding. Often a listener functions best when he is doing only that, without giving advice or making value judgments. At times you may become frustrated, and you are in great need of someone who will listen as you "let off a little steam."

Technical appreciation and challenge. You need someone in your particular profession or same type of work who can express appreciation of the work you are doing. Affirmation for a job well done is important. At the same time, it is vital that you have persons in your line of work who can critique your performance on the job and show you ways in which you can improve. In this way your work will not grow stale or superficial. It should be noted here that this appreciation and challenge to a worker can be done only by someone who knows about the certain field of endeavor. Also, it should be done by somebody whom you consider to be honest and trustworthy.

Emotional support and challenge. While a wife may not be able to give her husband much technical appreciation and challenge, she can give him a lot of emotional support. This means that she will stand by his side and support him, even if she does not always agree with everything he does. In fact, emotional support is extremely important for the wife to provide if the husband does not receive it on the job (as is often the case). As every husband knows, the relationship is quite reciprocal; the wife needs much emotional support, too, whether she works outside the home or not.

The other side of support is emotional challenge. There are times when you need to be confronted with your excuses and self-deceptions; someone must tell it "like it is." Many times the one friend who will do this is a greater friend than the one who will just merely listen to you.[9]

The social support system established with those around you can be very valuable. This system, though, does not have to degenerate into a constant griping session or crying time. You should not expect to receive continual technical appreciation on the job and never be challenged to do better. Your social support system, however, should help you to see life from a clearer viewpoint than if you did not interact with anyone at all. These persons should cause you to be honest with yourselves. And as you feel yourself pulling out of the burnout state, you should seek to make yourself available to others who need your help in the different areas outlined above. There are others of your acquaintance who are going through the same frustrations and problems you have encountered. Give to them the benefit of your experience; give *them* a helping hand. This is one of the underlying principles of such groups as Alcoholics Anonymous.

7. *For those in the helping professions: Seek to have the attitude of "detached concern" toward those you help.*

In an earlier chapter, the problems encountered by those in the helping professions were discussed. It was pointed out that the helper is often adversely affected by his contact with those he is trying to serve. This is true especially in situations in which the helper is continually confronted with hopeless or seemingly impossible situations. Human problems cannot be solved in the same way that mechanical or technical problems can, and this causes a high level of stress to exist in the helper.

Perhaps the most extreme example of this is the nurse who works with terminal cancer patients. When nurses first begin to work in the hospital with these patients, the tendency is to get emotionally involved with the patients and their tragic experience. Most nurses truly care about people, but people keep on dying. It is a truly hopeless situation. Nurses, without even realizing it, begin protecting themselves from being overwhelmed by the environment in which they serve. They pull away emotionally from the patients. Their detachment can be exhibited in several ways: resentment against the demands of the cancer victims; a kind of sick humor in which they mock the ones they care for; a false facade of valor which masks their feelings of helplessness, hopelessness, and resentment. Needless to say, the burnout rate among nurses in such situations is quite high.[10]

Emotional detachment from the problems of people can also occur among such helpers as pastors, counselors, and teachers. Sometimes the problems which people get themselves into are so strange and unnecessary that the natural tendency is to shake one's head and walk away.

People's confused lives and life situations appear almost humorous at times, if we forget that they are indeed very tragic. We pray for and with these individuals and claim the promises that God is able to work miracles. However, the months and years pass, and these people refuse to cooperate with divine help. They are still the same unchanged, mixed-up people they have always been. As someone said to me several years ago about a certain family: "Helping them is about as easy as unscrambling scrambled eggs!"

Teachers really want to see their students learn and get excited about the quest for knowledge. However, when Johnny and Linda refuse to do their homework and these children's parents do not seem to care either, what can the teacher do? The teacher has the choice of getting emotionally distraught about the apathy around him/her, or he can pull back, distance himself somewhat from the less-than-ideal situation, and do his best. That teacher must assume the attitude of "detached concern."

This is a balance which can be difficult to maintain. A professional helper must preserve a certain objectivity and detachment from those he or she wants to help. At the same time, he must demonstrate to the one being helped that he does care. He must show he is sensitive to the needs of those within his sphere of care and that he is concerned about their welfare. In attempting to practice detached concern, the professional helper fights dangers on both ends of the spectrum.

You can become overly involved in the situation and lose your objectivity. As one clinical psychologist so aptly described this danger: "Once you are in the shoes of your patient, you cannot be of any help. He has been in his shoes all along, and obviously has not done too well."[11] The opposite danger is complete detachment, which is characterized by a total loss of concern and a dehumanizing attitude. If you are too detached, you also cannot be of any help to anyone. Therefore, a proper balance of caring and detachment must be established and maintained.[12] Keeping these two factors in balance will lengthen your longevity as a helping professional and will keep your own personal life happier and more emotionally satisfying.

8. *Stay away from all false cures for burnout*.

Chapter six informed you that some solutions to burnout are not really solutions at all. The "cure" turns out to be worse than the disease itself. You can use many diversions and decoys, even self-destructive activities to mask your pain and help you forget. Do you cover up and camouflage, rather than reach out for a genuine cure? For a while you may feel better, but then you realize that your feelings of hopelessness and exhaustion remain. The false cures, if anything, have only made the burnout worse. Therefore, stay away from cures to burnout which cover up rather than get to the heart of the problem. Do not seek their help.[13]

9. *Determine that limit to which you can be loaded down with work and responsibility; do not let yourself go beyond that limit*.

Remember the example of the camel. This seemingly clumsy and homely creature is actually quite smart in one respect: he will carry a heavy burden, but he reaches a limit past which he refuses to go. His owner may try to sneak an added weight onto what the camel presently is carrying, but that only makes the camel balk and proclaim a sit-down strike until the burden is removed.

Many of us are not as smart as the camel. We have not yet learned what our "load limit" is. Despite our energetic natures, we are like the disciples: the spirit is willing, but the flesh is weak.

Our physical and emotional stamina does not equal our ambitious, go-getter spirit. We continue to accept responsibilities and projects which others are anxious to hand to us.[14]

Determining the limit of your work responsibilities and assignments is a personal matter; no one can make that determination for you. A few seem able to do this, and the results are disastrous if we try. We should not let the "workaholics" of the world make us feel guilty when we set limits to our work schedules and our activities.

Of course, the difficulty of putting this good advice into practice is that for most people, work responsibilities are imposed upon them from an external, higher source (simply speaking, the boss). Often we receive the ultimatum, "Do this—or else." In such situations, try adapting yourself to a heavier work load. Give yourself time to discover whether you can handle more or not. Or, positively yet firmly, stand up for your rights as a worker. Tell the employer you do not think you can handle a heavier load than what you are presently carrying. If the load is too heavy for you to bear, then begin looking for other employment. Always keep this in mind: No job is worth sacrificing your physical and emotional health in order to hold it.

Your load limit also should take into consideration your church and social life. You can be loaded down with too many heavy burdens even in these areas of life. The only difference here is that you have more latitude to say No than on the job. Of course, you should always be ready and willing to serve the Lord and your fellowman. However, your church life should never get to the point where it is viewed as another burdensome job to perform. Many have discovered that if they show a willingness to serve in the church, then a cascade of jobs and offices will come showering down upon them. This is especially true in smaller churches where often there are only one or two "church pillars" who are holding things together. Even in your church life, it is important to set a limit to your responsibilities and activities. You will then be able to perform your tasks with greater skill and cheerfulness.

10. *Disengage yourself from the working environment when you leave it.*

When you leave your work setting, really leave it, both physically and mentally. Don't bring a briefcase full of work home with you to labor over until midnight. Occasionally you may be forced into doing this, but you should make it a rare exception. Instead of bringing your job home with you, spend some quality time with your family; have fun together.

Some professionals have a problem with this coping principle because their work tends to infiltrate their total life-style. Two good examples are physicans and ministers. Generally, they are expected to be "on call" and be available when they are needed. I have been called away from a warm fireplace and a Scrabble game with my wife to help someone across town get his car started in 10° weather. I didn't feel like going, nor did I feel like the task especially fit my job description. However, they called me specifically, and it would not have been proper for me to say, "I'm not working now; I've already punched the clock. I can't be bothered." I wanted to reach this man spiritually, so I made myself available by helping him with an everyday problem.

In a very real sense, my work as a pastor touches practically all of my life. It is not possible to fit this work into a neat eight-to-five time slot. If you find yourself in a similar situation, you must creatively find ways to disengage yourself from the work environment. Seek to have one day a week where you can get your mind off that work completely. Deal with emergencies on that day, but nothing else. Consciously lay aside hours during the day for recreational activities and rest. If you don't, then your work will tend to overpower you. Also, consider the idea of the short retreat mentioned in the next chapter.[15]

Whatever you choose to do, make sure you do not allow yourself to work all of your waking hours. By doing that you are cheating yourself and your family. If you are not burned-out yet, such a schedule will cause you to be that way soon.

11. *Socialize with people outside your immediate work environment.*

If you are an attorney and all of your friends are attorneys, what do you think you will talk about when you all get together at a party or picnic? You guess it: the legal world! This is not to say that socializing with colleagues will necessarily promote burnout. As we learned in section 6 about support groups, it is important for peers who work together to compare notes, listen, give each other appreciation and advice, and perform other supportive functions. However, shop-talk can be stressful if it is always carried into the social arena. Make friends with people who are not a part of your work routine. Their social relationships with you will broaden your interests, and at the same time you will be able to get your mind off the problems and challenges you face at work.

12. *Utilize time management principles in governing your life.*

The great evangelist Fordyce M. Detamore had a valuable motto which he lived by: "Wasted Time Is Wasted Life." He taught it verbally and through experience to the ministers and other gospel workers who worked with him in his crusades. During his evangelistic work he would visit a large number of homes each day. His energy and dedication was a constant source of inspiration (and amazement!) to those who labored by his side. His ability to wisely use time is probably one of the keys to his successful career as an evangelist.

Time is certainly the stuff which life is made of. We all have been given the same amount of time in a day, no more and no less. If we waste a day, a week, a month, or a year, it can never be reclaimed. The wasting of time sets a pattern of chronic underachievement, a pattern which is difficult to break. A friend of mine recently gave an appraisal of one of his employees. It was exaggerated for the sake of humor, but it still had an element of truth: "That fellow gets to work at eleven, leaves at one, and takes an hour off for lunch."

The problem a lot of people have is not laziness. It is lack of organization. They accomplish little because they do not know how to use time in an efficient way. They waste time constantly, while believing they are busy. They tell others how rushed they are, but they have very little to show for their work, and this places them under much pressure. What many fail to realize is that wasting time and underachieving produces stress in conscientious people to the same extent as the work required for overachievement does.[16]

The overachieving person (the prime target for a burnout) tries to accomplish too much in too short a period of time. This person needs to adopt as his own motto "Put off till tomorrow some of the things which could be done today." Understanding how to set up a daily order of priorities with the use of a list will do much to liberate the overachiever from the work habits he or she has developed.[17]

Time management principles, therefore, will organize the disorganized person and retain the sanity of the overachiever. Space is limited, so it will not be possible to present an in-depth study of these principles. However, two excellent books about time management that I recommend most highly are *The Time Trap* by R. Alec Mackenzie and *How to Get Control of Your Time and Your Life* by Alan Lakein. Read them; you will learn a lot. To get you on the road to managing your time more effectively, here are the "Ten Commandments of Time Management" adapted from a newsletter sent to sales representatives:[18]

I. Analyze Your Time Use and Schedule It. Keep track of how you spend (and waste) time during the course a week; then use a daily planning book to schedule your time in the most effective manner for your lifestyle. In your book each day, establish a list of priorities of things to do that day. Do the most important things first, then the items of lesser importance.

II. Concentrate. Concentrate on doing one thing at a time, without jumping from one task to the other.

III. Take Breaks Away From Business. Recreation and family activities should have a place in your time schedule; these will clear your mind so that you will be able to concentrate better when you get back "down to business."

IV. Avoid Clutter. This applies to both the office and the time schedule! Do not try to schedule too much into a certain period of time.

V. Don't Be a Perfectionist. We should try to do our best, but remember that striving for perfection in our work is exhausting and wastes a lot of time.

VI. Learn to Say No. Learning to use this simple, short word is a great timesaver. It keeps you from doing things you don't want to do or don't have time to do.

VII. Don't Procrastinate. The longer you wait to accomplish an important, necessary task, the more difficult it will typically be for you.

VIII. Eliminate the Enjoyable Time-wasting Activities. The things we enjoy doing are often the reasons why we are kept from accomplishing something productive. This can also apply to "time robbers"—things not so enjoyable, but distracting anyway.

IX. Learn to Delegate. We are tempted to think we're the only ones who can do anything right. If we have this attitude, we will head toward energetic self-destruction; we will try to do everything ourselves. It is much better to teach others to do certain tasks so that we can be freed of having to do them.

X. Be Perceptive and Flexible. Don't make your schedule too rigid. Let changes occur whenever they are appropriate. Quite often, the needs of others must come before our well-planned schedules.

13. *Fight "Hurry Sickness"*

This principle is actually an extension of the fourth commandment found in the above list, but it is important that this "disease" be more fully highlighted and exposed. "Hurry sickness" occurs when you seek to schedule too much into a set period of time. Since time is inflexible, the only thing which changes is the speed of our activity. You give others the impression you are rushed and busy, because you are. They mention the fact that you are real "go-getters." However, your nonstop rushing around leads you finally into a dead-end street of exhaustion.

I mention "hurry sickness" because it is a tendency which I am constantly fighting. I wish I were the only one, but the freeways and sidewalks of our land reveal otherwise. There are many people hurrying to meetings which all began ten minutes ago. It happens to me this way: I know I have a business meeting scheduled for 7:30 p.m. However, at 5:00 I look at my yard and cringe at the tall grass. Instead of asking myself whether I have enough time to accomplish the task, I soon have my lawn mower whirring away. I have a fairly large lawn, so it takes about an hour and a half to mow. By 6:35 I have put the mower away, and I'm headed for the shower. While I'm in the shower, a member calls from another church and wants to talk about Vacation Bible School. I visit with her for a few minutes, but the watch on my arm silently reminds me that my time is running out. So, I gently ease out of the conversation, telling this woman that I'd appreciate being informed about all the latest VBS developments. I tell her I will call her back in several days. After finishing the shower, washing and blow-drying my hair, and getting into my suit, I jump into the car at 7:05. It is a twenty minute drive to the church. I know that I should have left fifteen minutes earlier, but "circumstances" just did not permit. Now I have allowed only five minutes leeway between the normal driving time and the appointed time of the meeting. And that twenty minutes does not allow for the unexpected freight train or traffic tie-up caused by an accident. (These unexpected tie-ups usually happen the very times we are running late, don't they?) Luckily, this time I arrive at the church for the meeting at 7:29. I silently promise myself I will never let it happen again.

Does this happen to you on a regular basis? Do you find yourself rushing to every engagement, only to find yourself late to about half of them? If so, then you have a habit on your hands which you need to break. You bring unnecessary pressure upon yourselves by cramming your schedules too full. In the above illustration, it would have been better to have mowed half of the yard or left it all until the next day. That way I could have had a relaxed time for supper, a warm shower, and a few minutes to look over the meeting's agenda. The next time you are scheduled to go somewhere to meet an individual or group of people, ask yourself these questions: Have I allowed myself enough time to get there without any undue pressure? What do I intend to do during the several hours before the meeting? Will it conflict with my later responsibility? If you ask these questions, it will help you tremendously. This may seem like a simple remedy, but it is an important one. "Hurry sickness" is one of the sparks which ignite a stressful life-style and leads a person eventually to feeling burned-out.

14. *Realize the shortcomings and weaknesses within yourself and others. Seek to hold down the perfectionist and idealist within yourself.*

An idealistic person is often a hostile and restless one. He knows the way things ought to be, or at least he thinks he knows. He wants others to conform to his ideal picture of the world and gets angry when they don't. Burned-out persons usually are idealists when they enter their professions. They start out with great hopes of changing the world. After a while they begin to realize that their environment is more resistant to change than they had dreamed. Certainly, idealism is a virtue if channeled in the right direction. The only problem is that the average work environment is far from ideal, and can be very frustrating at times.[19]

Idealism in young people is often reinforced by the academic world, which teaches students the way things should be in their chosen field of study. When they get out of school and into a job, they realize that the ideal set before them in college is not the way things actually are. Dr. Freudenberger in his book gives this example of a young lawyer who expects a precise world of theory and clear-cut precedents, but finds himself coping with shortcuts and expedients that were not in any of his legal textbooks. "He also finds himself dealing with confused, angry clients who want results and are not particularly interested in the ramifications of the law."[20]

The *perfectionist* is a close cousin of the *idealist*. This person works and works to get every aspect of his work and life just right, with absolutely no mistakes. A secretary will retype a letter if a typographical error is made or a student will drop out of a college class if the possibility of making a "B" exists. A perfectionist does not allow for mistakes and failures, either in himself or in others. When these shortcomings make themselves evident, this type of person is beside himself. He, too, gets frustrated very easily. Clyde Narramore describes him as "a busy bee who buzzes himself to distraction."[21]

You need to establish a standard of excellence and achievement for yourself. Do not be content with mediocrity. At the same time, remember you are in an imperfect world filled with imperfect and sometimes hard-headed people. They have weaknesses and shortcomings, and so do you. It sometimes pays not to take yourself too seriously.

15. *Get adequate amounts of exercise and recreation.*

Many positive results come from a consistent exercise/recreation program. One result not often mentioned is in the area of stress management. Exercise reduces the harmful effects of life's stresses and pressures. If stress is successfully managed in one's life, then burnout is less likely to occur. Since this is the subject of the next chapter, I point your attention there.

16. *Be nice to yourself: seek to maintain your health by following other established health principles. Pay particular attention to sleep and proper diet.*

The large majority of the population would feel "wiped out" and unable to function if they went for several weeks or months getting only three or four hours of sleep each night. It does not matter if they followed every other coping strategy in this or any other book. The simple truth is that everyone needs a certain amount of sleep. If you find yourself in the burned-out state, it may be because you are burning your candle at both ends!

Sleep repairs and restores the body. It helps conserve vitality so that you can awake refreshed. One author has stated it this way: "Sleep, nature's sweet restorer, invigorates the tired body and prepares it for the next day's duties."[22]

In fact we should pay attention to all eight of the natural remedies: "Pure air, sunlight, abstemiousness, rest, exercise, proper diet, the use of water, trust in divine power—these are the true remedies."[23]

These laws of good health are as relevant today as when they were first outlined eighty years ago. Perhaps they are even more applicable, considering the intemperance and less-than-desirable dietary habits of so many Americans. Whether you realize it or not, your health has a tremendous bearing upon how you are able to relate to the pressures and stresses of life. Clyde Narramore, in his book *How to Handle Pressure*, gives this dynamic illustration: "The weight of pressure is not only judged by the size of the load but by the strength of the one who bears it.

"A heavy crate can be carried by a large truck with ease, but that same crate when placed upon a child's wagon will crush it. The weaker wagon cannot sustain the heavy weight of pressure that is placed upon it. So it is with your physical well-being. When you suffer from poor health, you are overwhelmed by pressures that are not even considered as such by others who enjoy vibrant health. . . .

"People need stimulation in order to find motivation. Yet, when you're in a fragile physical state, any task demanding initiative becomes a stressful situation. Responsibility takes on the dimension of pressure. It doesn't take much to throw on the panic switch or cause you to crumble."[24]

17. *Seek to consolidate the "real you" with the image or facade which everyone sees you to be.*

This may seem like an abstract concept at first, but it is really important to understand. It is not unusual for individuals to project an image of themselves to the outside world which is quite different from what they are really like on the inside. People often play a role which they feel others expect from them. There are those who even set professional goals this way; they study to become a physician or lawyer because their father or some other family member has stereotyped them into this area. In reality, their interests lie in other fields of study. People hunger for approval from others, so they will erect false images and set false goals for themselves which they hope will be pleasing to everyone. At the same time, their "authentic self" keeps quiet. The moment of truth comes at some point, however; one's true self will be manifested. The person declares that he is tired of being a hypocrite and a phony. He just wants to be himself. This honesty usually does not manifest itself until a person has gone through a severe, trying crisis in his life.[25]

Of course, the image which you establish and which others see each day might actually be closer to the divine likeness than your true self. Your true, inner self might be almost totally opposed to

God's will for you. What is important to note is that this dichotomy is destructive. Leading a double life never works. Shakespeare wrote in *Hamlet*, "To thine own self be true." A basic honesty with ourselves and with those around us will prevent us from erecting a phony exterior which hides a totally different self inside.

18. *Develop emotional closeness with "significant others" in your life.*

Usually, there is a small circle of friends and family members whom you are able to particularly depend upon for emotional support when the going gets rough. You need them in normal times, of course, but their value to your life is magnified during dark, depressing periods. The individuals in support groups, at work, among friends, and at church often give us much help, but you should not attempt to develop an emotional bond with everyone you turn to for general encouragement and support. Only a few key individuals known in the psychological literature as "significant others," should share your innermost thoughts and feelings. It is with these persons that you should develop true emotional closeness. These often include a parent, one's spouse, a best friend or two, or a trusted advisor.

Of those in this list, your husband or wife should be the one with whom you develop the most emotional closeness and with whom you share the most intimate confidences. (Also, remember that confidences about one's homelife should not go outside the family circle.) The irony of all this is that many times you are emotionally distant from the ones with whom you should be the closest. Two major reasons exist for this dilemma: First, you are too afraid or too inhibited to tell your spouse how you truly feel, so you engage in much superficial conversation. Second, you never actively listen to what others are saying to you. Instead, you are only thinking up your response to their comments. If emotional closeness with those important people in your life is needed to keep you from burning out, then you should seek to tear down any and every barrier that would keep you from that closeness.[26]

19. *Spend time with yourself to reflect and think.*

While it is important to spend time with our families and close friends, you must not forget that you should seek time alone with yourself for tranquil, quiet reflection. Amid all of the activities of our lives, this is probably a rare occurence. You are around other people so much of the time in meetings, social occasions, and on the job itself. You reach a point where you grow weary of being around people. Some may disagree, but I believe it is vital on occasion to even get away for a few hours or a day from the spouse and the children so that you might think—alone. When was the last time you did something all by yourself, something you enjoy doing? It probably has been quite awhile.

Do you run away from thinking and self-reflection when you get all by yourself? Being alone may actually intimidate some. So what do you do? You flip through magazines and newspapers; you watch inane television programs; you keep busy with household chores. You do anything except come face-to-face with yourself.[27] I have caught myself listening to the radio constantly while traveling on long trips by myself. It did not matter what it was, just so it was something to listen to and absorb my thoughts. I've discovered that this is a form of running away from myself. Therefore, I leave the radio off during portions of these trips so that I can commune with myself, as well as with the Lord. I seek to cultivate the quality of "aloneness." Dag Hammarskjold once wrote: "The longest journey is the journey inwards."[28] He knew what he was talking about. Ellen White states it somewhat differently: "In order to receive help from Christ, we must realize our need. We must have a true knowledge of ourselves."[29]

20. *Get in touch with the source of lasting peace and strength.*

The Lord tells us in His Word, "I am the vine, ye are the branches: he that abideth in me, and I in him, the same bringeth forth much fruit: for without me ye can do nothing." John 15:5. These words are all-inclusive. There is no room for any doubt as to what Jesus means. He does not say, "You can do without Me on Wednesday and Thursday afternoons" or "You can find fulfillment apart from My presence during April and May." He states simply, "Without me ye can do nothing."

A number of coping strategies which counteract the effects of burnout upon one's life have been dealt with. I believe most, if not all, of the previous nineteen principles will benefit your lives if they are applied consistently. However, you will always sense that something is missing from your life if you do not establish and maintain a living connection with Jesus Christ, through the ministry of His Holy Spirit. The success and fulfillment you have searched for will continue to elude you. It will stay just outside your grasp.

Without help from an all-powerful God, the pressures and problems of life are able to overwhelm even the strongest of us. But with His help you will be able to move mountains: "I can do all things through Christ which strengtheneth me." Philippians 4:13. During the 1973-74 energy crisis, *Ministry* magazine published a cover story entitled "The Real Energy Crisis." The cover artwork showed a Bible with an electric socket built into it. The plug which had been in this socket was now disconnected. The point the magazine was trying to make is obvious: the real energy crisis in our lives is a spiritual one. We have been negligent in getting in touch with the source of power for our lives, and we have suffered as a result of this neglect.

My encounter with Christ has shown me that I must have Him dwelling in my life to supply the strength and inspiration I need for daily living. Whenever I have strayed from Christ during periods of my life, I have lost sight of life's true meaning. Many of you can also identify with that experience. If we are honest with ourselves, then we must agree with that old Negro spiritual: "If we ever needed the Lord before, we sure do need Him now!"

1. A number of the points in this chapter have been adapted from an article by Kevin Howse, "When the Pastor Burns Out," *Ministry*, April 1981. They have also been expanded to incorporate new concepts and material which are not included in that article.

2. Ayala Pines and Elliot Aronson, *Burnout: From Tedium to Personal Growth* (New York: Free Press, 1981), p. 10.

3. *Ibid.*, pp. 156-158.

4. *Ibid.*, p. 158.

5. Clyde Narramore, *How to Handle Pressure* (Wheaton, Illinois: Tyndale House, 1975), pp. 23-25.

6. Pines and Aronson, p. 11.

7. *Ibid.*, p. 122

8. *Ibid.*, p. 124.

9. *Ibid.*, p. 124-128.

10. *Ibid.*, pp. 4, 5.

11. *Ibid.*, p. 54.

12. *Ibid.*, pp. 54, 55.

13. Herbert J. Freudenberger with Geraldine Richelson, *Burnout: How to Beat the High Cost of Success* (New York: Bantam Books, 1981), pp. 100, 101.

14. Narramore, p. 39.

15. Kevin Howse, "When the Pastor Burns Out," *Ministry* April 1981, pp. 28,29 and Gary Collins, *You Can Profit From Stress* (Santa Ana, Calif.: Vision House, 1977), p. 53.

16. Howse, p. 29.

17. Alan Lakein, *How to Get Control of Your Time and Your Life* (New York: New American Library, 1973), pp. 63-68.

18. "If Time Is Money, Time Management Is Profit," *Shaklee Survey*, February 1981, p. 3.

19. Freudenberger, pp. 59, 60.

20. *Ibid.*, p. 60.

21. Narramore, p. 38.

22. Ellen G. White, *Child Guidance* (Nashville, Tenn.: Southern Publishing Assn., 1954), p. 342.

23. Ellen G. White, *The Ministry of Healing* (Mountain View, Calif.: Pacific Press Publishing Assn., 1905), p. 127.

24. Narramore, pp. 6, 7.

25. Freudenberger, pp. 26-29.

26. *Ibid.*, pp. 136, 137.

27. *Ibid.*, pp. 124-126.

28. Dag Hammarskjold, *Markings*, trans. Lerf Sjoberg and W. H . Auden (New York: Alfred A. Knopf, 1965), p. 58.

29. Ellen G. White, *The Ministry of Healing*, p. 455.

How to Keep Well

"Why are you so tired?" asked the wife, as her executive husband threw his suit coat onto the floor and collapsed on the bed. "All you've done today is sit in a meeting." Sam, the husband groaned. "If only you could have been at that meeting, you wouldn't be asking such a stupid question!"

The quarterly survey had been conducted that afternoon. Some of the statistics presented by the president of the company had not been very flattering. Sam's department especially was shown to be deficient in many areas. As the unfolding fiscal picture continued to worsen during the afternoon session, Sam felt the pressure mounting on his shoulders like a thousand-pound weight. The president's concluding speech had been especially sinister to him. "We did not do very well this past quarter, I'm afraid. We must see this situation turned around soon, or some of you might find yourselves without a job! Now, I don't like to threaten, but that's the way it is." Throughout the speech, the president kept looking at Sam. As he left the office that day, Sam felt like a total wreck. All he felt like doing was crashing into the bed as soon as he arrived at home, and that's exactly what he did.

Similar scenes are reenacted in the homes of America every afternoon. Job stress and strains are felt by practically all of us, and we wonder what we can do to keep our health and sanity—in spite of it all. Job stress, as we have learned, afflicts practically every job or profession. Even those employed in jobs which do not require much skill (such as fast food restaurants) are often subjected to stressful situations. Nurses and other health professionals often must endure high levels of stress as they care for the seriously ill. That there is no room for mistakes is a fact which constantly confronts them.

Administrators and executives also feel the burdens of stress. Although their work is sedentary, the mental and emotional stress of their professions causes them to grow physically tired. This is true of anyone who sits at a desk for eight hours daily. They are weary at the end of the day, but it is not the same type of weariness which the farmer will feel after working all day. The farmer, although he is physically exhausted, will feel relaxed and be able to enjoy a restful night of sleep. The executive, however, sits all day, working with figures and reports. He is using his mind and not his body. On top of that, the stress that he may experience from dealing with superiors, clients, and colleagues can be a very heavy load indeed. At the end of the day he will be very tired and uptight.[1]

Many of us are aware of the emotional impact which stress can have upon our systems, because these are the easiest symptoms to detect. We feel pressures coming upon us from various directions, and if we're not careful, stress can produce inside of us such destructive emotions as anger, bitterness, or despair. Unfortunately, a lot of people fail to realize that these unresolved tensions also exact a heavy toll upon their overall physical condition. If they were aware of this, perhaps they would make a more serious effort of managing their stress.

The chapter "Adding Fuel to the Flames" told us that stress causes adrenaline to be pumped into our bloodstream. At first glance, we might think this adrenaline is good for us, or at least harmless. However, along with this substance come fats (triglycerides), which end up being deposited upon the artery walls. We all know what that can eventually mean—strokes, heart attacks, and other life-threatening ailments. Isn't there some means by which we can short-circuit this process, so that the stresses of life will not be allowed to make us sick and permanently disabled? Physicians today are looking at physical exercise as the key. It is the escape valve which many people need in order to keep healthy and whole.[2]

Very often, we feel like doing only one thing after we get home from a hard day's work at the office: sitting down in an easy chair, eating our dinner from a nearby tray while we turn on the TV and hunt for some escapist entertainment to get our minds off of our problems. There is nothing wrong with a little "total relaxation" after a pressure-filled work day. However, if that is all we end up doing night after night, week after week, it is not healthful.

THE BENEFITS OF EXERCISE

Some physical exercise such as tennis, swimming, running and tossing a football in the park, or digging in the backyard garden will do wonders for the worker who finds himself "stressed-out." A number of health authorities are saying today that vigorous walking—a mile or more per day—is perhaps the best form of exercise for the average American. If you are in doubt about the type of exercise you can engage in, be sure to consult your physician.

But exercise is the very last thing you may want to do when you are so tired. Remember that you are tired from mental and emotional stress, and not physical exertion. Once you begin your exercise routine, the demands of the physical activity will diminish the impact of this tension-producing stress upon your body. Your muscles will have a chance to stretch and relax, and the end result is relaxed nerves. Thirty minutes of moderate exercise daily can help melt away hours of nervous tension. Of course, the hours of nervous tension are unhealthful for us, and we cannot look to exercise as a magic cure-all. It will, however, *minimize* the effects of an unhealthful, stressful work environment and overall life-style. While we should be seeking an appropriate exercise program for ourselves, let's not forget to initiate reforms in our overall life-styles which will reduce our stress levels.

What benefits can we hope to gain from a program of daily exercise? If planned well, it should give the heart and complete cardiovascular system added strength and vigor. It will also burn up the excess amounts of adrenaline in the bloodstream which have accumulated due to stress. Certainly, this will provide a long-term health advantage.[3] Exercise changes fat weight into lean weight, and it tones up weak, flabby muscle tissues so they can work more efficiently. The body's total blood volume increases, which means more oxygen and nourishment will go directly to the body tissues. The psychological effects of regular exercise can be substantial also, because when one feels and looks better, the self-image and whole outlook on life improves.[4]

For those who have trouble losing weight, physiologists have good news: they believe now that exercise adjusts the body's rate of metabolism, so that one's "inner thermostat" is turned up considerably if he or she exercises regularly. So, an exercise enthusiast is less likely to gain excess pounds than his nonexercising friend is prone to do. This theory goes on to state that our bodies develop a *setpoint*—a weight level to which the body naturally adjusts itself. This explains why it is so difficult to lose weight by most diet methods and then keep it off. Scientists believe exercise causes this setpoint to be lowered, so that the body and its metabolism process is comfortable with a lower body weight. A full explanation of the Setpoint Theory may be found in *The Dieter's Dilemma* by Dr. William Bennett and Joel Gurin.

We're all familiar with the phrase "the flabby American." For some of us, the phrase strikes home a little closer than we would like it to. Being overweight and out of physical condition are two of the greatest menaces to the health and well-being of Americans today. In fact, over 60 percent of all American adults are overweight, and this state lends itself naturally to a whole range of degenerate diseases, especially as we grow older.[5] This out-of-shape, flabby-American syndrome also contributes to the overall "burned-out" feeling people are complaining about today. Can we really expect it to be otherwise?

Fortunately for us, certain commonsense programs of exercise and diet have been developed during the past twenty years. These programs, if followed faithfully, will restore both the physical condition and the proper weight. The aerobics program, developed by Dr. Kenneth Cooper in the mid-1960s, takes a scientific approach to exercise. In his books he explains aerobics in depth. His research has found that for a person to be fully conditioned, he needs to consume 1680 milliliters of oxygen per week during a given space of exercise time. In order to make it easier for the average person, Cooper developed the point system. The "training effect," his term for conditioning, begins in one's fitness program when he consistently earns thirty points per week.[6] The man or woman exercising can reach this state of conditioning through a wide variety of activities: swimming, running, cycling, walking, basketball, stationary running. Charts on each of these activities are included in Cooper's books, showing how many points can be earned for a particular workout. I prefer to earn my thirty points each week by swimming half a mile, three times a week, at the local YMCA, and then walking two miles, twice a week. When I follow this program faithfully, it makes me feel great; every aspect of my daily routine seems to run smoother. Of course, like daily devotionals, it is an ongoing struggle to be regular and consistent with this exercise program.

THE BENEFITS OF DIET

Along with Dr. Cooper's aerobics exercise program, I'd like to recommend the writings of Nathan Pritikin in the area of diet. Some feel his approach to nutrition is severe and exacting, but his ideas make more sense than the multitude of fad diets flooding the market today. His book *The Pritikin Permanent Weight-Loss Manual* is very informative. The main premise of the book is that a diet high in complex carbohydrates, high in fiber, and low in fats and sugar will assist a person in achieving the weight level he or she desires. The right exercise program, combined with a sensible, nonfattening diet, can mean only one thing: before long, there will be a new, more healthy and happy *You*.

THE BENEFIT OF GETTING AWAY FROM IT ALL

Along with a daily exercise routine, stretches of time for extended relaxation and recreation are needed by today's worker. Some engaged in the study of burnout and stress believe that three or four four-day vacations interspersed throughout the year probably have a more beneficial effect upon the worker's emotional well-being than a two-week vacation taken all at once during the summer. If you are not able to use your vacation time in this way, you should seek periodically to take weekend vacations.

Find an out-of-the-way place outdoors, one where you will not get involved in another traffic jam to get there. Pitch your tent underneath a big, shady tree beside a gurgling brook. (Sounds like paradise, doesn't it?) Do those things which you never seem to have time to do—look at the flowers, skip rocks in the brook, take your dog for a walk. There's no need to miss out on your worship service on vacation weekends; simply find the church of your choice in a nearby town. Of course on occasion it is good to have your worship service just as a family out in nature. That can be quite inspiring. By the time Sunday evening arrives, you will be amazed how relaxed you are. Drive back home early enough on Sunday evening so that you can get a restful night's sleep and can be ready to face life's battles come Monday morning.

You may be saying, "But I don't know of any relaxing nature spots where I can escape for a weekend. The only pretty places I know of are overrun with people." This may be true, but with a little persistent hunting and perhaps some detective work, you'll be able to find that perfect getaway spot. A friend might have a cabin in the woods which he might let you rent.

A change of scenery, whether it is for a few days or even for just a few hours, usually gives to you a new perspective upon life which you need very badly. The problems will more than likely still be there when you return, but your *perception* of those problems might be different as a result of a change of scenery. And often that makes all the difference in the world. A simple picnic, a trip to the zoo, a jaunt to the mountains, desert, or beach will provide to you what some describe as "decompression"—the opportunity to unwind and release yourself from some of the built-up pressures you have been accumulating.[7] In 1867 Ellen White gave this prescription to a group of institutional workers, which is quite similar to the one I gave you: "Let several families living in a city or village unite and leave the occupations which have taxed them physically and mentally, and make an excursion into the country, to the side of a fine lake, or to a nice grove where the scenery of nature is beautiful. . . . The ride, the exercise, and the scenery will quicken the appetite, and they can enjoy a repast which kings might envy."

She then tells us the results of such recreational activities: "Exercise in the open air for those whose employment has been within doors and sedentary will be beneficial to health. All who can should feel it a duty to pursue this course. Nothing will be lost, but much gained. They can return to their occupations with new life and new courage to engage in their labors with zeal, and they are better prepared to resist disease."[8]

Our recreation and relaxation can take a myriad of forms. We may belong to a health club and enjoy going there several times a week to work out with the different types of body-building equipment. We may have a flair for music and enjoy having friends over on Saturday evening for a fun-filled singing-and-playing session. Some folks derive a great deal of relaxation from such nature activities as bird-watching and insect-collecting. They can do it for hours, while others (like myself) would enjoy it for only about thirty minutes. I've known those who unwind with such diverse hobbies as cabinet making, coin and stamp collecting, restoring antique cars, or writing poetry. All of these hobbies and activities help break the monotony and routine of daily living, which cause (at least in part) the burned-out state. All work and no play—what a draining experience for the human system!

Make sure that the recreation you engage in is true to its name. Be certain your activity is "re-creating" your physical, emotional, and mental strength, rather than depleting it. There are amusements which promote escaping from reality. These amusements are counterfeits for the real remedies available for the burdened-down person. Often they cause you to be more weary and emotionally drained than when you started. To top it off, many amusements are addictive in nature. They excite one's nervous system. Like any false cure for burnout, these amusements appear for a while to reduce the pain, but then the burnout is intensified by that activity. It spreads farther and farther, rather than being stopped.[9]

There is a world of difference between the amusements found in our world today and the invitation Jesus once gave to His disciples: "Come ye yourselves apart into a desert place, and rest a while." Mark 6:31. One will build up our strength, while the other ultimately will tear down. Every one of us is in great need of genuine rest, so that we might be able to withstand the pressures of life. Exercise, rest, and recreation: these are valuable protections against burnout.

What are *you* doing in your life to lessen the effects of stress? Are you winning or losing the battle? The following test (page 90) has been developed which pinpoints different coping strategies you should be utilizing to avoid burnout. Also, it mentions four different life-style habits which have a negative impact upon one's stress level and overall health. By taking this test you can see more accurately how you are coping with the pressures and the stresses of life which inevitably come our way.

STRESS TEST/COPING STRATEGIES

The test following was developed by George S. Everly, Jr., for the U.S. Department of Health and Human Services.

_____ 1. Give yourself 10 points if you feel that you have a supportive family around you.

_____ 2. Give yourself 10 points if you actively pursue a hobby.

_____ 3. Give yourself 10 points if you belong to some social or activity group that meets at least once a month (other than your family).

_____ 4. Give yourself 15 points if you are within five pounds of your "ideal" body weight, considering your height and bone structure.

_____ 5. Give yourself 15 points if you practice some form of "deep relaxation" at least three times a week. Deep relaxation exercises include meditation, imagery, etc.

_____ 6. Give yourself 5 points for each time you exercise thirty minutes or longer during the course of an average week.

_____ 7. Give yourself 5 points for each nutritionally balanced and wholesome meal you consume during the course of an average day.

_____ 8. Give yourself 5 points if you do something that you really enjoy which is "just for you" during the course of an average week.

_____ 9. Give yourself 10 points if you have some place in your home that you can go in order to relax and/or be by yourself.

_____10. Give yourself 10 points if you practice time management techniques in your daily life.

_____11. Subtract 10 points for each pack of cigarettes you smoke during the course of an average day.

_____12. Subtract 10 points for each evening during the course of an average week that you take any form of medication or chemical substance (including alcohol) to reduce your anxiety or just calm you down.

_____13. Subtract 5 points for each evening during the course of an average week that you take any form of medication or chemical substance (including alcohol) to help you sleep.

_____14. Subtract 5 points for each evening during the course of an average week that you bring work home; work that was meant to be done at your place of employment.

Calculate your total score. A "perfect" score would be 115 points. If you score in the 50 to 60 point range you probably have an adequate collection of coping strategies for most common sources of stress. However, you should keep in mind that the higher your score the greater your ability to cope with stress in an effective and healthful manner.

1. Clyde Narramore, *How to Handle Pressure* (Wheaton, Illinois: Tyndale House, 1975), pp. 101-103.

2. *Ibid.*, pp. 102, 103.

3. Gary Collins, *You Can Profit From Stress* (Santa Ana, Calif.: Vision House, 1977), pp. 208, 209.

4. Kenneth Cooper, *Aerobics* (New York: Bantam Books, 1968), pp. 12, 13.

5. Nathan Pritikin, *The Pritikin Permanent Weight-Loss Manual* (New York: Bantam Books, 1981), p. 21.

6. Cooper, pp. 24, 25.

7. Collins, p. 53.

8. Ellen G. White, *The Adventist Home,* (Nashville, Tenn.: Southern Publishing Assn., 1951), pp. 501, 502.

9. Herbert J. Freudenberger with Geraldine Richelson, *Burnout: How to Beat the High Cost of Success* (New York: Bantam Books, 1981), p. 104.

Jesus' Answer to Burnout

When I was in college I attended a free lecture on transcendental meditation. Curiosity was my main motive in attending. The poster advertising the meeting showed the picture of the bearded mystic Maharishi Mahesh Yogi, and it declared, "Inner happiness is the basis for successful and fulfilling activity." I couldn't agree more, so I went.

The lecturer that afternoon told the assembled listeners that many, many beneficial things resulted from this practice. The speaker showed charts describing how it decreased people's anxiety levels and blood pressure; increased the rate of intellectual growth and perceptual ability; reduced the use of alcohol, cigarettes, and drugs of all kinds. Meditation, the speaker said, would improve mental and physical health, job performance, and satisfaction of workers; indeed, it promised to improve the overall well-being and inner peace of everyone who practiced it faithfully.[1]

The grandest claim of all could be found in the brochure which the speaker distributed: If the technique of transcendental meditation was implemented by all governments on every level, it would *"eliminate the age-old problems of mankind in this generation."*[2] Following the lecture, the speaker said that we all could learn the specific technique of this path to inner tranquility; that is, if we would pay him $125. Practically the entire group assembled there rushed up to him and signed up.

These were sincere, intelligent young people, looking for happiness and peace of mind, as well as freedom from mental anguish and the crushing weight of modern stress. Who could blame them for seeking a solution to the confusing and troubling problems constantly thrown in their pathway? The lives of many today could be summed up in the words which Shakespeare once used to describe our earthly existence: "a tale told by an idiot, full of sound and fury, signifying nothing."

We all want that inner tranquility and contentment which transcendental meditation promises to us. Wars and conflicts may rage unabated in many places of the world, but we all know where the greatest battles are being fought: inside of our hearts. The forces of light and darkness, good and evil, are constantly struggling to control our hearts and minds. How we long for answers so that we can make some sense out of life!

While transcendental meditation is promoted as a "definite, systematic technique" and not based upon any philosophy or religion,[3] its relationship to eastern mysticism is quite obvious to the Christian. He cannot practice this technique because in doing so he would be embracing a thinly veiled form of Hinduism. Still the question remains: Why does it work for people?

As I walked out of the lecture that afternoon, I was astounded by the claims made by the speaker and wondered whether all the charts and graphs were actually true. Then this thought came to me: "It might be that what he said is all true. But if I practiced transcendental meditation, I wouldn't need a Saviour, because it claims to do for me all that Christianity promises—and more. I would be able to solve all my problems and inadequacies myself. And I'm sure that's what Satan would love for me to believe."

BASIC SIMILARITIES
The practice of looking into oneself to find a solution to the problems and struggles of life is not confined to transcendental meditation. In fact, Americans are turning to all kinds of quasi-religions and the human-potential movements in hopes of "finding themselves." Some of these movements include Silva Mind Control, Self-realization, yoga, encounter groups, est, Zen Buddhism, the Hare Krishna movement, Scientology, and Psychosynthesis to name a few.[4] While differing greatly in their outward appear-

ances, they share several basic similarities.

They believe that "stress is bad and should be eliminated." We must remember that our goal is to manage stress, not be lulled into a state of complete relaxation and inactivity. They "dull our thinking and open up our minds to harmful influences." Eastern meditation does not point our minds toward elevating subjects, but encourages us to empty our minds of all thoughts, except its "mantra." These practices "elevate man and deny the need for any experience with God." They teach that we are all potential deities, so God is not needed in eliminating our stress and solving our problems. They "desensitize the conscience and promise happiness without facing the issues of sin."[5]

The multitude of counterfeit spiritual solutions to life's problems only make evident to us the hunger of soul being experienced today by people. Unfortunately, the "spiritual" answers they often find are as empty as their own lives. These paths to spiritual enlightenment turn out to be darkened, dead-end streets.

But for all of the counterfeit solutions to people's problems, there must be the genuine article. Many of us have discovered that solution and where it comes from—the Creator God, the Lord of heaven and earth. Only His solution is complete, and lasting.

A friend of mine recently gave me a plaque which reads, "God is greater than any of my problems." That's a dynamic statement! Think about that for a moment. God has spiritual resources at His disposal to heal the darkest depression or burnout that any of us might have. Paul writes, "My God shall supply *all your needs* according to his riches in glory by Christ Jesus." Philippians 4:19. Emphasis supplied. He is able to restore us to the state of happiness and inner joy we once experienced, if we are willing to cooperate with Him.

THE COMPLETE ANSWER

God is our Creator, and He knows how we should function best, both in our minds and in our bodies. If we follow His plan, as outlined to us in His Holy Scriptures, then we will stay healthy, happy, holy, and contented. If we don't, then we'll suffer from the many and varied effects which come as a result of deviating from that divine plan. Burnout is just one manifestation of the sin problem that has been plaguing the human race for 6000 years. For that reason, only God can provide the complete answer.

Our great objective in life is not to "find ourselves" through years of anxious self-discovery. Rather, we should seek to "lose ourselves" in a life of unselfish service for God and our fellowman, a life that ever grows closer to the heavenly Father. Jesus once profoundly stated this concept: "He who has found his life shall lose it: and he that loseth his life for my sake shall find it." Matthew 10:39. We "lose ourselves" in order to find life's true aim and purpose—the kingdom of God. If we do this, says Jesus, every aspect of living will be enriched beyond our wildest imaginations: "But seek ye first the kingdom of God, and his righteousness; and all these things shall be added unto you." Matthew 6:33.

THE GOSPEL'S SOLUTION

Practically everyone of us has heard the gospel story. We've read of how men and women became sinners many years ago through disobedience to God. We've heard about the amazing provision which the heavenly Father made to save the human race: He sent His own Son down to this earth to become a man, take on human flesh, and finally offer Himself as a sacrifice upon the cross of Calvary. An actual member of the Godhead died so that we might have the chance to live. "God sent not his Son into the world to condemn the world; but that the world through him might be saved." John 3:17. Preachers have told us that we can have the assurance of living forever with God in a newly created earth, if we will accept, through faith, the free gift of His grace into our lives. Perhaps some of us have become "gospel-hardened" because we've heard it so many times. For a lot of people, the Christian message and the new life it promises is intangible and hard to grasp. They find it full of abstract jargon and symbolism. Unfortunately, there are those who have been in the church for thirty years who still have not looked past these intangibles and abstractions to develop a relationship with Jesus.

So, if you've never become a Christian, it could be you've never been able to arrive at the essence of the gospel. In all honesty you ask, "What does a tragic event 2000 years ago have to do with my life today? How will the gospel message help me pay the mountain of bills I owe or find me a decent job when I'm in the unemployment line? How can the words in a holy book restore my happiness and peace of mind and give my life the direction it needs?" These are legitimate questions, and don't feel guilty if at times you find yourself asking them. On the other hand, it is not fair to raise such questions unless you are willing to give Christ and His gospel a chance in your life.

What exactly can the gospel of Jesus Christ do for my life *today*? And what can He do for me so that I might be able to escape from the burnout trap? I could say a lot at this point, but instead I'll share with you the thoughts of Dr. Anthony Campolo. In his message *Ministry in a Secular Society*, he brings into focus the benefits one experiences in the Christ-filled life: "Jesus came into the world in order to equip me to live life with full aliveness. But two things keep me from living life with full aliveness and intensity in the here-and-now: they are guilt and anxiety. Guilt keeps me in the past; anxiety keeps me in the future. These are the two maladies of modern people. They suffer from guilt, which is carrying the burden of the past; anxiety is living with a fear of the future. But if all of your energies are sucked up in the past and the future, you have no energy with which to live *now*."

"The good news of the gospel is that Jesus will approach you here and now and deliver you from guilt and anxiety. And when He does that, you will be free for the first time in your life from these weights which so easily beset us. We will be free to live this moment with fullness. And Jesus came, says the Scriptures, that you might have life, and have it more abundantly. (See John 10:10.) His gift is offered not just so that we might go to heaven. He wants you to live life *now* with abundance, to live every moment of every day with the fullness of its potential."[6]

Do you want to live a full, abundant life-style? I invite you to become a follower and disciple of Jesus Christ. Some complain that the Christian life is drab, dull, uninteresting, and restrictive. They say this because they have never truly experienced what it means to live "in Christ." They've received a false impression about Christian living from some professed Christians, perhaps, and this has turned them off. What these folks don't realize is that the Christian life is not a dull and lifeless drudgery which takes away your freedom. Instead, it is "the greatest adventure open to mortal man."[7]

While on this earth, Christ showed to us what a life in harmony with God's principles is like and what it can accomplish. Christ gave us the perfect example of spirit-filled living, of dependence upon our heavenly Father. Not once did He depend upon His own power; Christ always looked to His Father for strength and guidance. By a surface reading of the gospel story, some might think Christ's life and ministry were a failure. However, His life is the greatest success story ever recorded. No other life has had quite the impact upon the lives of others and the affairs of mankind as that solitary life. Through beholding that life in the Scriptures, we can grasp the ideal life God has established for us—one of fulfillment, success, inner strength of character, and dependence upon Him.

Today, Jesus Christ is engaged in a special work for us. He is in the heavenly sanctuary, standing there as our High Priest, Advocate, and Elder Brother. Scripture tells us: "There is one God, and one mediator between God and men, the man Christ Jesus." 1 Timothy 2:5. Christ encourages us to enter into the restored relationship with God *through* Him. In Hebrews, Paul exhorts us, "Let us then with confidence draw near to the throne of grace, that we may receive mercy and find grace to help in time of need." Hebrews 4:16, RSV. We have immediate access, twenty-four hours a day, to the throne room of God. Heaven's powerful resources are available to us through the direct connection we have with Christ. Never do we get a busy signal, nor do we have our prayers received by a celestial answering service. Instead, we talk directly to our Mediator, who then relays the burdens of our hearts to His Father. If you believe in the reality of prayer, think of the potential it has in relieving the stresses of modern living. The psalmist invites us to "cast thy burden upon the Lord, and he shall sustain thee: he shall never suffer the righteous to be moved." Psalm 55:22. How superior is the activity of prayer when compared with the mindless mantra one chants to himself in transcendental meditation.

The many promises which result from God's amazing grace are woven through the Bible like the bright, colorful threads in a beautiful tapestry. First of all, Christ's relationship with man causes us to become adopted into God's great family. "But as many as received him, to them gave he *power* to become the sons of God, even to them that believe on his name." John 1:12. Emphasis supplied. This adoption process into the family of God gives to our lives a holy power never before available. Also, it means we are never alone. Unseen heavenly angels are always nearby to give us assistance in time of need. Fellow Christians in the body of Christ are there to lift us up during times of discouragement and depression.

The experience of having Christ dwell within our lives gives to us a restfulness and peace which is not available from any other source. With the calm assurance gained from daily fellowship with Christ, burnout fades away. We do not need to be in a state of restlessness and uncertainty any longer. With His mighty arms He lifts the burdens of stress and pressure off our shoulders and bears them Himself. In their place He gives us peace. "Peace I leave with you, my peace I give unto you: not as the world giveth, give I unto you. Let not your heart be troubled, neither let it be afraid." John 14:27. Matthew's Gospel repeats this promise in a beautiful way: "Come unto me, all ye that labour and are heavy laden, and I will give you rest. Take my yoke upon you, and learn of me; for I am meek and lowly in heart: and ye shall find rest unto your souls. For my yoke is easy, and my burden is light." Matthew 11:28-30.

What wonderful promises! That's what we're looking for—rest and peace. This is not a transient, temporary feeling, not the empty bliss of the Hindu nirvana, but enduring peace and happiness. Of all the solutions given previously for relieving the burned-out state, Christ provides us the ultimate solution.

In one of her inspiring devotional books, Ellen G. White comments upon this reality: "A life in Christ is a life of restfulness. There may be no ecstacy of feeling, but there should be an abiding, peaceful trust. Your hope is not in yourself; it is in Christ.

Your weakness is united to His strength, your ignorance to His wisdom, your frailty to His enduring might."[8] "Abiding peace, true rest of spirit, has but one Source. . . . *This peace is not something that He gives apart from Himself.* It is in Christ, and we can receive it only by rceiving Him."[9]

Accepting Christ means that He will give to us a new nature. "If any man be in Christ, he is a new creature: old things are passed away; behold, all things are become new." 2 Corinthians 5:17. A person without Christ can change objectionable outward behavior. He can even attempt to alter negative thought patterns through "positive thinking." There is one thing we are incapable of doing, however; we cannot, by ourselves, change our basic human natures, from which flow bad actions and bad thinking. We need divine help; we need the indwelling Christ, with His personal representative, the Holy Spirit, to bring about this transformation. With Their presence in our lives, we can become "more than conquerors." See Romans 8:37. "The Christian's life is not a modification or improvement of the old, but a transformation of nature. There is a death to self and sin, and a new life altogether. The change can be brought about only by the effectual working of the Holy Spirit."[10]

OUR COOPERATION IS NEEDED

The promise of the Holy Spirit working in our lives is a very precious one. He is sent to us from heaven so that He might be our special Helper throughout life. The close relationship we can have with the Spirit is made evident by Paul when he describes our bodies as the temple, the very dwelling place of the Holy Spirit. Because of Christ's love to us, the Spirit is sent to be our Helper, Teacher, and Comforter. This Comforter makes life bearable in a world filled with tension, sadness, and turmoil. We are able, through the Spirit, to live above the world's problems. At the same time we are enabled to be a functioning, productive member of society, doing something to ease some of the suffering which surrounds us.

Before we can experience all of these wonderful realities, however, we must be willing to respond to heaven's invitation. Christ tells us in Revelation 3:20: "Behold, I stand at the door, and knock: if any man hear my voice, and open the door, I will come in to him, and will sup with him, and he with me." There is a role for us to play in our salvation. *We* must open the door. In Matthew 11:28, 29, Christ promises rest for our souls. For this to happen, though, we must respond to Him. He says, "Come unto me. . . . Take my yoke upon you, and learn of me." The Holy Spirit gives to us the initial desire to come to Christ. If we don't resist this invitation, then we will be drawn to Him.

What does it mean to "come to Christ" and "give my heart to Him"? It means accepting Him as both my Saviour and Lord. I must be willing to surrender myself to the will of God so that the rest of this life will be spent living the way He wants me to live. In surrendering my heart to God, I'm surrendering, not to an enemy, but to a friend. I'm saying, "Lord, I want to accept the grace made possible to me through the death of Jesus on the cross. And as Jesus gave Himself fully to God's will in self-surrender upon the cross, so I want to give my life totally to You today. Take every aspect of my life—my work, my spare time, my family, my beliefs, attitudes and thoughts, my tastes and interests—and mold them into what You would have them to be."

Perhaps you are saying to yourself, "That sounds nice, but I'm not ready to make such a commitment to God. I don't want to surrender!" If you are that honest with yourself and with God, then you're not too far away from Him, if you allow yourself to be led by His Spirit. Make this your earnest prayer: "Lord, make me willing to be made willing to surrender to You."[11]

As you can see, coming to Christ in repentance and surrender is not a mere gimmick or technique to help us feel good quickly. Instead, it involves the giving of our total self to God. The paradox of the gospel is this: salvation is a free gift, something we are incapable of earning or deserving. At the same time, the gospel means that we give everything we possess to the lordship of Jesus Christ. This lordship does not result in slavery, but is the greatest freedom we could ever experience.

Surrendering our hearts to Jesus leads to our justification, where our pseudo-goodness is exchanged for the perfect righteousness of Christ. We stand in the sight of God as if we had never sinned. As our lives become a clean slate, thanks to the merits of Christ's righteousness, we realize the promise given by the apostle Paul: "Therefore being justified by faith, we have *peace with God* through our Lord Jesus Christ." Romans 5:1. Emphasis supplied. Isn't this our great need in this life?

Morris Venden, in his book *How to Make Christianity Real,* asks, "How do we surrender?"

"First of all, we must have a desire for something better than what we are presently experiencing. This desire cannot be self-generated; it can only come from God, Christ, and the Holy Spirit.

"Next we must gain a knowledge of the plan of salvation. This is something that God will not force us to learn; we have to place ourselves in the environment in which that happens—wherever His Word is read, spoken, or taught.

"The third step in coming to Christ is admitting that we've been running, trying to escape from Him through all sorts of ways. If we take a long look at ourselves, we'll have to recognize our sinful condition.

"The final step in coming to Christ is the hardest of all. . . . We must acknowledge that we have no ability to change ourselves. Although God is running after us, He can't help us until we are at the point of great need. And just like the prodigal son, we don't usually come to Jesus until we get to the end of our own resources. As one writer has said, 'The Lord can do nothing toward the recovery of man until, convinced of his own weakness, and stripped of all self-sufficiency, he yields himself to the control of God. Then he can receive the gift that God is waiting to bestow. From the soul that feels his need, nothing is withheld.'—*The Desire of Ages,* p. 300."[12]

KEEPING THE FIRE ALIVE

Usually, a new Christian is excited about the new life he has found. He cannot keep quiet or still; the joy within his heart is incapable of being held in. After this initial joy and happiness, however, we find too many new Christians growing discouraged and silent. Their "first love" experience becomes cold. Some even abandon the faith completely, saying, "Well, I guess this Christianity business promised more than it actually delivered."

Is it possible to keep the fire within our hearts alive as the weeks, months, and years of life unfold? Of course it's possible. Jesus wouldn't bring us to the point of the new birth and justification, give us newfound rest and peace, and then abandon us. The Lord provides us six components of the Christian life so that our experience can be as fresh and exciting as the day we were baptized. If we make these components of Christianity a solid part of our lives, then we will have the best available protection against burnout. Prayer, Bible Study, Christian Meditation, Fellowship With Christian Believers, Witnessing to Others of God's Goodness, and Keeping the Sabbath—these are the six best protections against burnout.

PRAYER

Prayer has been described as "the opening of the heart to God as to a friend."[13] What a privilege, if we will only avail ourselves of this opportunity. The benefits of social support systems were mentioned earlier. However, here is the greatest support system one could ever have. "Prayer is the key in the hand of faith to unlock heaven's storehouse, where are treasured the boundless resources of Omnipotence."[14] If we desire "boundless resources" with which to live a full life, this is the first place we should go! Let's never get the feeling that prayer is an optional activity, though. Our spiritual life depends upon prayer in much the same way as our physical life depends upon the breathing of good, clean air.

BIBLE STUDY

While prayer allows us to speak to God, Bible reading and meditation makes it possible for God to speak to our hearts and minds. A thoughtful hour spent each day reading and contemplating the life of Christ and other uplifting biblical subjects will bring a startling transformation in our daily experience. The failure to do so causes us to stay in our old, familiar rut. Says Billy Graham in *Peace With God*, "Ninety-five percent of the difficulties you will experience as a Christian can be traced to a lack of Bible study and reading."[15] Think about that next time your mind is beset with anxiety, resentment, and jealousy. Don't give yourself a guilt complex, but calmly ask yourself this question on a daily basis, "Have I eaten from the Bread of Life today with the same eagerness as I have eaten my physical food?"

Satan will use everything in the world to keep us from studying the Word. He will even use the Lord's work! Therefore, we should not try to *find* time for personal devotions; we have to *make* time for this essential activity and let nothing else crowd in. Most people who have an ongoing, vital devotional time each day have discovered that early in the morning is the best time to spend with God. In this early-morning period, we can gain strength for the day's battles and trials. Don Hawley is so right when he says, "To gain a final victory over us [Satan] does not have to talk us into committing some great crime. All he has to do is keep us busy."[16]

Of course, the theme of our daily study is so important. We can use our Bible-study time to learn historical facts or to prove other people's beliefs wrong, and such study will never cause us to progress spiritually. But if we make Jesus and His righteousness the focus of our study, then He will give us power to live a victorious, Christlike life. "The reception of the Word, the Bread from Heaven, is declared to be the reception of Christ Himself. As the Word of God is received into the soul, we partake of the flesh and blood of the Son of God. . . . The written Word introduces the searcher to the flesh and blood of the Son of God, and through obedience to that Word, he becomes a partaker of the divine nature. As the necessity for temporal food cannot be supplied by once partaking of it, so the Word of God must be daily eaten to supply the spiritual necessities."[17]

CHRISTIAN MEDITATION

Christian meditation is tied closely to Bible study and prayer. This activity is an almost forgotten art among Christians. It is a time of contemplation and reflection—a time to think quietly about what you've said to the Lord in prayer and what He has said to you in Bible study. It means spending periods of time alone with God.[18] One can profitably spend time meditating on the beauties of nature, because this is God's "second book." A "Christian meditator" will also contemplate the plan of salvation and all that is true and noble, just and pure, lovable and gracious. See Philippians 4:8, NEB. As we think on these things, our lives will reflect those virtues.

A commitment to Christian meditation means that we will do more than quickly read a "thought for the day" as we gulp down our orange juice. On the other hand our lives were not meant to be spent solely in prayer, Bible study, and meditation. Life was not meant to be spent in a monastery. Someone has wisely observed that "he who does nothing but pray will soon cease to pray."[19]

FELLOWSHIP WITH BELIEVERS AND WITNESSING

Jesus' answer to burnout involves even more than the three components of Christian living we've just examined. As a result of renewal in our relationship to God, our fellowship with Christian believers will be renewed. We will long to spend time with them in worship, study, and prayer. We will want to socialize and make friends with those whose lives are pointed in the same direction as ours.

Because our lives will be brimming with God's love, we will want to share that love with those around us. We might want to become involved in some organized church outreach or community service program—not because we feel pushed into it, but because it brings us great joy. As many of us know, Christian witnessing helps build up our own courage and strength, as well as benefiting the person we have witnessed to. If we commit ourselves to a life-style of serving our fellowman, our own personal problems have a way of growing smaller.

KEEPING THE SABBATH

Then there is the Sabbath, a weekly memorial to God's creative work. The Sabbath is a celebration of God's goodness, a special time which comes to us every seven days. The spiritual, mental, and physical rest available to mankind on the Sabbath would do much toward eliminating burnout's many symptoms if people the world over kept it holy. The Sabbath is a special gift from God, a gift we would be wise to cherish and appreciate. It is a covenant sign between God and His children, and it lets them know to whom they truly belong. Christian Sabbath keepers know who is their Creator and who is the Lord and Master of their lives. In addition, the Sabbath provides a twenty-four-hour period to stop and think, to examine the course our lives are taking. It is a brief interlude in the maddening rush of daily affairs so that we might have some quality time to spend in inner stillness. The batteries which have run down during the week are allowed to recharge. The Lord knows the human system is prone to burnout; that's one of the reasons He invites us to enter into the Sabbath rest with Him. Every area of our lives is enriched by this weekly encounter with the Lord upon the Sabbath.

Burnout threatens the lives and well-being of an untold number of persons in today's industrialized, urban, fast-paced society. However, we can see that the spiritual resources provided by the Lord are, by themselves, more than sufficient to permit us to experience life with full aliveness and intensity. If you consider yourself to be one of burnout's victims, be sure that you give the Lord a chance in your life. He is able to transform even the most wretched and hopeless of life situations into something beautiful.

1. See *Fundamentals of Progress* (Maharishi International University, 1975)

2. *Ibid*., p. 54.

3. *Ibid*., p. 51.

4. Gary Collins, *You Can Profit From Stress* (Santa Ana, Calif.: Vision House, 1977), p. 184.

5. *Ibid*., pp. 197, 198.

6. Anthony Campolo, *Ministry in a Secular Society* (tape), Andrews University, September 1979.

7. Don Hawley, *Getting It All Together: Victory in Christ Now* (Washington, D.C.: Review and Herald, 1974), p. 79.

8. Ellen G. White, *Steps to Christ* (Mountain View, Calif.: Pacific Press Publishing Assn., 1956), p. 70.

9. Ellen G. White, *The Ministry of Healing* (Mountain View, Calif.: Pacific Press Publishing Assn., 1905) p. 247. Emphasis supplied.

10. Ellen G. White, *The Desire of Ages* (Mountain View, Calif.: Pacific Press Publishing Assn., 1898), p. 172.

11. Thomas A. Davis, *How to Be a Victorious Christian* (Washington, D.C.: Review and Herald, 1975), pp. 59-79. (two chapters on surrender)

12. Morris Venden, *How to Make Christianity Real* (Arroyo Grande, Calif.: Concerned Communications, 1982) pp. 46-48.

13. White, *Steps to Christ*, p. 93.

14. *Ibid.*, pp. 94, 95.

15. Billy Graham, *Peace With God* (New York: Doubleday and Co., 1953), p. 151.

16. Hawley, *Getting It All Together: Victory in Christ Now,* p. 41.

17. Ellen G. White, "Connection With Christ," *Review and Herald*, November 23, 1897.

18. Lynn Sauls, *TM or CM?* (Mountain View, Calif.: Pacific Press Publishing Assn., 1977), pp. 7-10, 18-20.

19. White, *Steps to Christ*, p. 101.

For Further Reading

Chalmers, Elden and Esther. *Making the Most of Family Living*. Mountain View, Calif.: Pacific Press, 1979.

Collins, Gary. *You Can Profit From Stress*. Santa Ana, Calif.: Vision House Publishers. 1977.

Cooper, Kenneth H. *Aerobics*. New York: Bantam Books, 1968.

Davis, Thomas. *How to Be a Victorious Christian*. Washington, D.C.: Review and Herald, 1975.

Freudenberger, Herbert J., with Richelson, Geraldine. *Burnout: How to Beat the High Cost of Success*. New York: Bantam Books, 1981.

Hawley, Don. *Getting It All Together: Victory in Christ Now*. Washington, D.C.: Review and Herald, 1974.

La Haye, Tim. *How to Win Over Depression*. Grand Rapids: Mich.: Zondervan, 1974.

Lakein, Alan. *How to Get Control of Your Time and Your Life*. New York: New American Library, 1973.

McQuade, Walter, and Aikman, Ann. *Stress: What It Is; What It Can Do to Your Health; How to Fight Back*. New York: Bantam Books, 1974.

Machlowitz, Marilyn. *Workaholics: Living With Them, Working With Them*. New York: New American Library, 1980.

Mackenzie, R. Alec. *The Time Trap*. New York: McGraw-Hill, 1972.

Narramore, Clyde, and Narramore, Ruth. *How to Handle Pressure*. Wheaton, Ill: Tyndale House, 1975.

Osborne, Cecil. *The Art of Understanding Yourself*. Grand Rapids, Mich.: Zondervan Publishing, 1967.

Pelletier, Kenneth. *Mind as Healer/Mind as Slayer*. New York: Dell Publishing, 1977.

Pines, Ayala, and Aronson, Elliot. *Burnout: From Tedium to Personal Growth*. New York: Free Press, 1981.

Pritikin, Nathan. *The Pritikin Permanent Weight-Loss Manual*. New York: Bantam Books, 1981.

Selye, Hans. *Stress Without Distress*. New York: New American Library, 1974.

Tournier, Paul. *The Healing of Persons*. New York: Harper and Row, 1965. (especially chapter 9—''Overwork and Idleness'')

Walton, Lewis, and Douglass, Herbert. *How to Survive the '80s,* Mountain View, Calif.: Pacific Press, 1983.

White, Ellen. *Life at Its Best,* Mountain View, Calif.: Pacific Press, 1964.